S0-AAC-530

HOT HITS, CHEAP DEMOS

The Real-World Guide

to Music Business Success

Nadine Condon

Backbeat
Books

San Francisco

Published by Backbeat Books
600 Harrison Street, San Francisco, CA 94107
www.backbeatbooks.com
email: books@musicplayer.com

An imprint of the Music Player Network
Publishers of *Guitar Player, Bass Player, Keyboard,* and other magazines
United Entertainment Media, Inc.
A CMP Information company

CMP
United Business Media

Copyright © 2003 by Nadine Condon. All rights reserved. No part of this book
covered by copyrights hereon may be reproduced or copied in any manner whatsoever
without written permission, except in the case of brief quotations embodied in articles
and reviews. For information, contact the publishers.

Distributed to the book trade in the US and Canada by
Publishers Group West, 1700 Fourth Street, Berkeley, CA 94710

Distributed to the music trade in the US and Canada by
Hal Leonard Publishing, P.O. Box 13819, Milwaukee, WI 53213

Cover and text design by Michael Cutter

Library of Congress Cataloging-in-Publication Data

Condon, Nadine, 1951–
    Hot hits, cheap demos : the real-world guide to music business success /
    by Nadine Condon
    p. cm.
    Includes index.
    ISBN 0-87930-762-5 (alk. paper)
    1. Popular music—Vocational guidance. 2. Music trade. I. Title.

ML3795.C649 2003
780'.23'73–dc22

                                                                    2003052393

Printed in the United States of America

03 04 05 06 07   5 4 3 2 1

Dedication

For Honey

TABLE OF CONTENTS

Introduction
Who Needs This Book… and Why

If you are a musician, you need this book. Regardless of your musical persuasion, this is the *one* book that will save you *money, time,* and *heartache.*

It doesn't matter if you are just starting out or are established, if you're in mid-life, mid-career, or mid-teens, or if you're a high school or post-college performer. Whether you're an electric, acoustic, or computer-oriented musician, whether you want a major label record deal or are wondering if a music career is even in the cards for you—*if you write, record, or perform music,* from mixing it in the bedroom to selling it in the boardroom, you will benefit from the power of this book.

As an artist development specialist with 14 gold and platinum records from appreciative friends and clients, I can attest to the make-or-break factors in careers. I know what works for creatives, regardless of their musical genres. And unlike some other old schoolers, I still continue to discover, promote, coach, befriend, and help guide the current generation of superstar musicians and their business partners.

I've based this book on what I've seen work *firsthand,* not classroom theory. You will see—through true stories of other successful musicians—what works and what doesn't. Remember this one little truth: Everyone you hear on the radio today or watch on MTV was once exactly *where you are right now* in your career! Same doubts, same frustrations, same challenges.

Because I know musicians, this is *not* some text-dense book written in that foreign language called "legalese." I've written this book in the same practical, down-to-earth style you've become familiar with in my seminars. The format is easy to read and *to the point*, since no one has the time to wade through useless, irrelevant information.

I'll tell you the real secrets of artist development and why every overnight success is *years* in the making. I'll help you ask yourself pertinent professional and creative questions honestly. I'll show all musicians the steps to having a long, rewarding career while enjoying the process, regardless of musical genre or background.

This book will help you see the value of possibility, identify resources, and keep focused on successful strategies for music goals *you* define. I will explain the balance between art and commerce, why your business is as creative as your music, and the simple steps you can take to have a successful career on your own terms. The same talents that make you a dynamite singer, songwriter, or player are the same talents you will use in your business strategies.

I have over 20 years' experience dealing intimately with the wildest and most creative musicians of my generation. I have personally worked for, produced showcases for, or mentored musicians who have gone on to sell over thirty million records during the last 25 years, remained on the *Billboard* 200 music charts for over 500 weeks, appeared on every major award show, and toured four continents.

But it's through my four-day music festival, Nadine's Wild Weekend, and my unsigned band showcases that I've come to most appreciate the efforts musicians make to put their talent out there. I've seen great bands self-destruct and mediocre bands hit the charts. Working so closely with talent, I want to share what I know to be tried-and-true for creative people. As I told the *San Francisco Chronicle* recently, I started writing this book because "no one tells the truth about the music business." Information is knowledge. The more you know, the more you can free yourself up to create your best works!

My career has been filled with thousands of bands and the camaraderie of many creative people on both sides of the fence—in music and in business. I've watched many *possibilities* become *realities*. With so little respect shown for artist development in today's commercial music climate, this book is dedicated to all musicians—aspiring or established—who are willing to reach and maintain their potential.

Whether it's playing the Viper Room in L.A., standing up at open mic night in Chicago, or writing a lullaby for your child, you will find the creative process to be the foundation of your (life's) success.

Don't be overwhelmed. Recognize the potential that exists for you every single day. Open your eyes to the *possibility* and succeed!

Nadine Condon
San Francisco Bay Area

1

Shape Your Future

Introduction: The Power of Possibility

If you are serious about a music career, forget about production points, production deals, record deals, major labels versus indie labels, rip-offs, one-offs, radio airplay (or lack of radio airplay), selling out, commercial bands versus alternative bands, solo artists, Triple A (Adult Album Alternative), pop, rock, country, Hot AC (Adult Contemporary), good managers, bad managers, legal versus illegal online downloads, and the intrinsically evil necessity of attorneys. Forget about whether the business is selling or not selling records, perpetrates an antiquated, outmoded marketing system, or is in the midst of the most significant marketing revolution of the twenty-first century.

Instead, concentrate only on *your* definition of success, and what you can do *immediately* that will have a tangible effect and move you toward your goals. Everything else will flow from those two simple actions. There is always *one* concrete step you can take that will bring you that one step closer to your dreams.

The music business is overwhelming to artists because it's a big, amorphous, unmanageable animal. The vagaries of the music business are both confounding and confusing. Once you think you've got a line on it, the rules change. Historically, it's been like this forever, so don't think you have it any harder in the 2000s than in other decades.

Of course that, to me, is the appeal. I love the music business for everything it is and isn't. It's not confining or rigid. It has few rules. Sometimes it's not nice. Sometimes it's maddening. Most often it's clueless. It has little regard for artist development. It lurches along, semi out of control, relying on luck and happenstance. But always, always, always living and breathing with *possibility.*

It's this *possibility* that is intoxicating and addictive. It's this *possibility* that gives me an adrenaline rush when I hear a new song, see an innovative band, or meet a brilliant young musician who challenges my sensibilities. It's this *possibility* that keeps folks of all ages taking chances. It's this *possibility* that makes you sneak into the bathroom in the middle of the night to write just one more song. It's this *possibility* that keeps the playing field level and opportunity right around the corner.

The biggest secret in the business is that the No. 1 problem facing all artists is not the big bad music industry. The No. 1 problem is that artists get frustrated, break up their bands, and stop writing songs, performing, and recording. If you surrender to frustration, you deny yourself the *possibility* of living out your dreams. You deny yourself the *possibility* of a thrilling musical career, gold and platinum records, and the ability to touch millions of people with your muse. Everyone gets overwhelmed because success seems so far away. But personal success is made up of very simple little actions strung together by making good choices and knowing what you want to accomplish before you start out.

This chapter will explore the bricks of a good artistic foundation and end with a real world story about one of my favorite rock role models: Melissa Etheridge. You'll see that respecting your artistic muse, realizing your power of choice, defining your goals, and evaluating your artistic capabilities are the personal commitments that will allow your unique talents to develop. Your creativity cannot

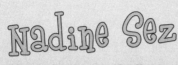

Nadine Sez

Music business challenges

Although the circumstances have differed over the decades, the music business has always been and remains challenging.

In the early days there was no music business as we currently know it. Musicians sold records out of the trunks of their cars. The industry was oriented toward Top 40 singles and run by a handful of men in New York and Los Angeles. Competition was very different, with far, far fewer releases. There was much less radio availability, and "race" records (music made by black artists) couldn't get played on the radio—nor could country music. The venue situation for live performances was, then as now, problematic. Radio, then TV, gave music a widespread boost, creating a demand for manufacturing and distribution. But distribution was local and regional based. The criteria for success seemed to be a matter of persistence, hard work, luck, and timing.

Today there is no music business as we currently know it. Singles—now sold over the Internet instead of out of musicians' cars—are back in vogue. The industry is oriented toward radio airplay in specific genres and run by a handful of multinationals in New York and Los Angeles. Competition is very intense, with too, too many releases. There is much less radio availability, and independent records (music made by unsigned artists) can't get played on commercial radio. The venue situation is, now as then, problematic. Distribution, now as then, remains spotty (which is why the Internet has become such a powerful tool). The criteria for success seem to be a matter of persistence, hard work, luck, and timing.

The best way to handle things is to give yourself as much education and information on how current music business is conducted. If you want a career today, it may mean looking at it differently and more seriously than your contemporaries would have in the past.

exist without you feeding it, nurturing it, and tending to its needs. Those needs are as unique as your talents. The more you recognize what makes your talent special, the better able you will be to make your creativity work for you.

Call Yourself an Artist

Many, many people are conflicted in their approach to making music, singing, or songwriting. They try to please everyone in their life, whether it's their boss, girlfriend or boyfriend, grandparents, or band mates, and they only end up straddling the fence, exhausted from being pulled in so many different directions. Too afraid to make a commitment to their muse, they spend their lives day-dreaming and living as what Julia Cameron in her book *The Artist's Way: A Spiritual Path to Higher Creativity* calls "shadow artists," dependent on the artistic efforts of others.

If you are going to respect yourself enough to put energy into your music project, you should be able to tell yourself you are an artist. Focused energy is more efficient than being pulled in many conflicting directions and ending up pleasing no one, especially yourself. When you determine to respect your artistic muse and step into the role wholeheartedly, much of your conflict will be resolved. It's not that other people won't accept us in these roles; it's ourselves that can't accept us in these roles. However, others treat us reflective of how we treat ourselves. If *you* treat your goals respect-fully, others will start treating them that way too.

It doesn't mean you shouldn't hold a steady job, remain in a com-mitted relationship, or go to the folks' for Sunday dinner. It does mean *defining yourself accurately.* If you don't start defining yourself accurately, how will other artists know you are out there? How else can they find you, in collaboration, in support, and in camaraderie? Don't forget, people are "attracted" to other like-minded people, and musicians are no exception.

Make a commitment to yourself by taking the first step of calling yourself a musician. Your creative expression is the language of your soul, and *your* soul only. No one else's. It won't matter if you change your mind down the line about your career, or if things do not work out how you originally envisioned, because you're working only to your specifications. The only person that will be judging your efforts is you.

It's your power of choice that will define your notion of success and failure and what constitutes those definitions. Once you realize that *it's all within your control* a lot of pressure is off your back, mentally and emotionally, and you can make your first efforts. As far as your art is concerned only *you* are the real judge of your commitment to exploring your interior talents. Allow yourself to *explore!*

Make Appropriate Choices

Your power lies in making choices that will help you succeed. Ultimately, you have the power to say yes or no. Writing a new song, practicing your instrument, or rehearsing your act are all examples of things *you* decide. Developing alternative venues, researching college radio, and developing a Web site are all decisions *you* make. Whether you want to take responsibility or not, everyone chooses how to spend their free time. Once you remember that you control your decisions, you can define your success criteria, make a commitment to them, and determine what effort is needed to achieve them. You won't be as concerned over what may or may not happen, because you will be too busy with what *is* happening. And once you start something in motion, the law of physics and your subconscious power of intention will generally keep it moving forward.

A common distraction is that others will always try to tell you what you should do. If you truly know what you're seeking and why, you won't be easily thrown off course by often clashing "advice." Whatever makes you happy and keeps you actively pursuing your craft is going to be how you define success—not what works for that speed metal rap band in the rehearsal hall three doors down.

When you are rejected or feel thwarted in your efforts, you have choices of how to respond. One is to accept the fact that you did as well as you could and leave it at that. The other is to go back and find that *unique delivery* that demands a reaction from listeners. It's your choice how—or even if—to continue. It's not my judgment call nor the A&R rep's call nor the booking agent's call. It's your call. That's your power and responsibility to yourself.

You can determine what is going to go on around you by making good choices. Choices that support your needs. Choices that give you options. Choices that are appropriate to you. Be aware and conscious of what is going on around you. Can you really write about someone else's experiences in a different value system? This is why there are so many one-hit wonders. You can't make yourself something you're not. Your value system and the structure of your life are the underpinnings of your career.

You know yourself best and your instincts are always right. Trust yourself! You're the coach, quarterback, wide receiver, and punter. Don't follow someone else's game plan. If calling a club booker scares you, then wait and do it later when you are more confident and buoyed by some recent successes. Make decisions based on what you *can* accomplish.

22 Actions You Can Take Right Now

1. You *can* buy a notebook to jot down lyric and gig ideas.
2. You *can* advertise in a weekly to find a band.
3. You *can* put a band together.
4. You *can* find a spot to rehearse.
5. You *can* carve a rehearsal schedule out of your time.
6. You *can* write a new song.
7. You *can* buy a small recorder to record riffs while commuting.
8. You *can* rehearse productively.
9. You *can* build a Web site.
10. You *can* research appropriate clubs.
11. You *can* contact those clubs.
12. You *can* book a good show.
13. You *can* publicize your show.
14. You *can* send out an e-mail to your fans about the show.
15. You *can* make a poster for the show.
16. You *can* research recording studios.
17. You *can* research producers and engineers.
18. You *can* hire a producer.
19. You *can* record a demo.
20. You *can* get your demo reviewed.
21. You *can* send out postcards about the demo.
22. You *can* play a free show.

Define Success for Yourself

This is homework. Make a list of what you think you want to do. Think as big as possible and don't limit yourself in the beginning. (Your dreams are part of your creative language.) Think about what it is that rewards you. Is it audience feedback or simply wrestling a cranky bridge into submission? Is it seeing yourself on MTV or is it simply playing the hot local club on a Saturday night? Do you want to have fun for the next few years before you "grow up" or do you want a 25-year career? Is it more satisfying writing solo music or do you enjoy the challenge of collaboration?

By defining your success and strategy, you replace whining about

 **Nadine Sez**

You are the content providers

Whenever you are depressed and feeling small, and are certain you are so clueless that you will never figure anything out, remember you are the *content providers* of the entire entertainment business. The entertainment business can not exist without you. So despite the seemingly overwhelming odds, don't give your power away. *They* need *you*.

Don't feel restricted to one career path, since there is no *one* way to succeed. Don't base your career on what works for someone else. Steal, beg, and borrow information from lots of different sources but apply only what works for you. Instead of judging your activities on what Led Zeppelin or the Sex Pistols might have done, create new ways of thinking appropriate to today. Your business is going to be as unique as your music. Don't waste time on things that may be appropriate for others but not for you.

Don't set goals that are dependent on the actions of others. If you do, you will still be waiting for them to act! Your music is the one thing you must own solely. You can't expect others to feel the same attachment to your goals. Don't forget you have powerful new tools at hand (Internet promotion, alternative distribution, and indie labels) to assist you in establishing your measure as an artist.

the business with the simple steps you can take that will get you closer to your dreams. You may not have a songwriting organization in your region, but you can sit down two nights a week to practice songwriting for a national competition. You may not be able to get that club booker on the phone, but you can research 15 club addresses to receive your demo package. You may be out of money and can't afford studio time, but you can record your live shows through the house PA system.

When you know the reasons you are playing music and what pushes your buttons, it will be easier to formulate how to get what you want. If you're content having fun, drinking beer, and hanging out, why stress out over an expensive, inappropriate recording? If you want to sell your records to millions of people, you'll be better able to deep-six that band mate that doesn't approach the music as seriously.

Not everyone is meant for mass commercial success. Simply writing a compatible chorus or having the courage to stand up at open mic night may be enough to satisfy your creative longings. Be realistic as to what kind of "career" you want to work toward, and know in advance the criteria demanded by that format.

Evaluate Your Capabilities

Evaluating your art realistically is the hardest thing for an artist to do, since everyone thinks their singing is great, their playing is great, their songwriting is great. But it is necessary to learn how to evaluate your music in the realistic context of *the type of success* you are seeking.

Some levels of success may demand sacrifices you are unwilling or unable to make. Determine what you are willing *and* able to do to meet your satisfaction goals. This will go a long way toward preventing you from becoming disillusioned and frustrated down the line.

Be realistic, so that the goals you set are attainable. Know in advance what criteria are currently demanded in your chosen format of success. You may have to *write* songs in a *certain* style, *record* in a *particular* manner, *perform* in a *specific* way, and *sell* by a *mandated* method to attain explicit forms of success. Not everyone is willing to compromise themselves in the ways demanded for widespread "commercial" success.

Recognize what avenues are open to you and be smart about it. If you are an acoustic ballad writer, joining a songwriting association may be more appropriate for your aspirations than getting airtime on the local show on your city's hard rock stations. If you are dying to tour, partnering with other road bands will be a lot more rewarding than bands constricted by 9-to-5 jobs.

Ask Yourself Two Questions

There are two questions to ask yourself when trying to determine whether your music is on par with what you are seeking:

1. **Is my music getting a response?**
2. **Do things keep happening that keep the project moving along?**

These two questions apply to every situation, regardless of genre and style. Do you like the music you are creating? Do you like it enough to keep creating, practicing, and performing? Are interesting possibilities opening up to you? Do venues call you back? Do songwriters contact you? Does another band want to play with you? Did your rehearsal hall extend your lease? Did a garage open up for practice? Did you meet a studio owner willing to give you some recording time? Did you find a bass player just when your other one quit?

If your songs do not get a response or your options seem to have dried up, you may have to make some changes and try other avenues. Be open and flexible. Don't frustrate yourself by being unrealistic about things. Not everyone has superstar talent.

If your music is getting a lukewarm reaction, then you may not be exhibiting the talent necessary to get recognized. This may mean you don't have the talent, or that you have not found the appropriate expression that conveys your music effectively. In any case, be honest with yourself. Your music may be the best thing that you've ever done, but that doesn't mean it is up to current professional standards. If your instinct says to swim upstream against the popular grain with your music, fine. But know that by doing this, your success may take on different characteristics.

Create Your Signature Sound

One reason every overnight success is years in the making is because it takes that long for you to listen to your own voice and create a musical identity that is uniquely yours. Discovering the things that make you stand apart from the crowd is generally a time-consuming process of filtration while you try on and test different personae. Whether it's your delivery of the song, your original arrangement of the music, your stage presence, or your recording style, this uniqueness is *your currency as an artist.*

While arguably all music is derivative to some degree, it's how you fuse your musical influences from other records, the radio, MTV, and the Internet into your personal sound. Create a new sound. *Do not* rip off the Beatles, the Stones, or Radiohead—we've already heard them. If you're going to copy other bands, it's much wiser to copy indie bands that are not getting played on the radio. Remember, it's not how much you sound *like* other successful acts, it's how *different* you sound from them. Every successful act has an identifiable sound. When you hear them on the radio, you know immediately who it is, even if you don't know the particular song. Successful bands have strong, simple, easy-to-understand identities. White Stripes, Black Flag, the Strokes, Wilco, Elvis (both of them), Neil Young, Bowie, U2, Pearl Jam, Madonna, Bruce Springsteen, the Ramones, Melissa Etheridge, Peggy Lee, Coldplay—all come to mind as artists with highly recognizable identities.

Constant re-evaluation means deliberate analysis of who you are, what your sound is, what your music is, and what's working. Every step of your career should be helping you refine your artistic message. Every successful artist has usually developed and discarded several different personae and projects before they hit on the right combination. Everyone remembers his or her first demos. Those old demos are not who you are today. The steps you take along the way—refining, defining, and focusing on your talents—will be the groundwork of your career.

Stick with It and Give It Time

Since *every* artist you hear on the radio today was once exactly where you are right this minute in your career, then *every* artist you admire also had to go through humiliating periods of self doubt, musical styles that were not working, and periods of seemingly no forward movement. Everyone has to make bad music before they make good music.

The art of popular music (possibly an oxymoron) is the most demanding of careers to develop. It's big, bulky, and dependent on a host of outside resources necessary for creative evolution. No other genre of art requires a band, instruments, equipment, PA, studios, clubs, and audiences to progress. Also no other art form insists that its practitioners be responsible for a commercial bottom line, like bars and nightclubs insist for musicians. These realities make it the hardest of all art forms to master successfully. Knowing in advance the possible time commitment will let your talents emerge more significantly.

Nadine Sez

The artist development debate

Some industry insiders are disgusted with me because they think I'm too encouraging to mediocre talent. Some artists think I'm too harsh in my demanding criteria for widespread commercial success and that I sell out. I stand by my commitment to artist development. No one starts out great. You can have brilliant talent, but unless you choose to develop it in an effective (and affective) way, that talent has no currency in today's climate. I've seen many, many artists with good talent reach inside and challenge themselves to develop to their highest potential. This often means being realistic enough to surround yourself with a team of players and business associates who can enhance what you are doing more effectively.

Most music I hear is good but not great. I hear very few great artists today. If I get a hundred demos, maybe eight to ten might garner slight industry interest. Out of those, one to three may have potential to "make it." For those, the chances they will actually go on to get a major label deal and *sell records* are less than ten percent. That's how high the criteria are for major labels.

Most musicians put the cart before the horse and worry about playing RFK Stadium before they've mastered the basics. Instead of being worried about what *might* be, concentrate on what *is*. Do you have a capable instrument? Do you have your tools—a small notebook or tape recorder to track your riffs and lyrics outside of practice time? Have you written your first song? Do you have the time set aside to devote to songwriting? Do you have collaborators? If not, have you searched musician-based chat rooms on the Internet?

Each time you accomplish something proactive (setting a rehearsal date and following through, or putting a good bill together for the club show), acknowledge your efforts. The more you concentrate on what you *can* do, you'll feel more in control of your destiny and less of the debilitating frustrations that generally lead to a band breaking up.

Chapter 1 Keywords

1. Break down the "impossible" into **simple steps** of feasible activity.

Old friends: Manager Bill Leopold and Melissa Etheridge with me backstage at the KFOG Christmas concert in San Francisco, 2001. Melissa found success by staying true to herself.

2. Remember you have the power of **choice** to say yes or no to every action.
3. **Stick with it** and give yourself a chance.

Chapter 2 will show you how to make a plan that serves as the catalyst for your continuing efforts and brings you closer to your goals.

REAL-WORLD SUCCESS STORY:

Melissa Etheridge

Melissa Etheridge is one performer who embodies just about every great trait demanded of artistic and commercial success. She has a signature sound, style, and personality. She performed and wrote songs for years, refining her style, before she broke through to mass success. She's had to re-evaluate her career realistically on occasion. And she has created a support system of management and crew that allows her to link her personal and professional goals.

Melissa was discovered far off the beaten path in Long Beach, California, by Karla and Bill Leopold. Shortly thereafter, Bill Leopold formally took over her management duties. Initially, labels were not interested in Melissa, so he negotiated a publishing contract with Rondor Music (Almo-Irving) that gave her some money to live on while she developed her songwriting skills. Several years later, a record producer who knew Island Records' head honcho Chris Blackwell took Blackwell out to see Melissa in Long Beach. (The producer, Dino Aureli, didn't have a car he thought was nice enough for Blackwell, so he borrowed his friend Dino Barbis's car). Regardless of the mode of transportation, Chris "got" Melissa and signed her on the spot, with Leopold negotiating. Although she was raw and undeveloped, Blackwell knew she was a unique and passionate entertainer.

Armed with an album's worth of material, Melissa went to San Francisco a few years later to record her first record at the famed Record Plant. The finished product was a very produced, very polished pop record. (It even had strings.) But as everyone knows by now, Melissa's not a pop singer. She's a dynamic rocker, often compared to Bruce Springsteen in the intensity of her shows.

Blackwell hated the record. He took his favorite picture of Melissa, put it on the studio console, and told her to make an album like "that." The picture (which later became the album cover) was vibrant and conveyed her unique singular strength and conviction.

So Melissa scrapped that first effort. She went back and recorded the whole first album in just seven days, with her own team of players. She recorded almost everything "live to track" with very few overdubs. The record brimmed with emotion and power. The song "Bring Me Some Water" showcased her talents perfectly. This debut record went on to sell over half a million copies (gold record status) and launched her into the beginning stages of superstardom.

I had the good fortune to do quite a bit of promotional work with Island Records in the late '80s to early '90s. They had no field staff, and all their promotional work was contracted out. I worked on all of Melissa's early tours. Recently, when I was moving, I found early tour itineraries and even an early demo tape of hers that Island had sent me in 1987. It had a rough cut of "Bring Me Some Water," still one of my favorite songs. Even on that little cassette tape, it was obvious that song was special.

The first time I saw Melissa live was at the Gavin radio convention showcase in San Francisco at a then brand-new nightclub called Slim's. The room was wall-to-wall people, and there was a tangible air of "happening." I went with my two promotion friends from Island Records, Andy Allen and Bob Catania. Squeezing through the front door, we proceeded to witness two hours of high voltage rock 'n' roll, unlike anything I had previously seen. Melissa poured her heart and soul into every song, singing and playing with a seemingly abandoned passion. The concert was like a baptism, revival, and greatest date of your life, all rolled into one. I was soaked in sweat and emotionally wrung out at the end, all pretense of cool professionalism cast aside, cheering and stomping for more.

Melissa is a great example of someone who had a plan, but the plan didn't work out as anticipated. She was able to roll with the punches, be flexible, and make adjustments. She made a new plan but always kept her goal in sight. She trusted her instincts.

Melissa Etheridge has always been a class act. From day one she has treated her fans, her support staff, and the music industry with the utmost respect. Not only does she still maintain a long-standing tradition of pre-show "meet and greet" time, she has now taken over the actual concert promotion of many of her own shows. When I worked promoting her records, she never complained, no matter how many radio stations or record stores I asked her to visit, despite her demanding concert schedule.

Melissa's support staff is exemplary. She has one of the finest management teams I've ever seen, still led by Bill Leopold. They not only adhere to her value system, they enhance it. They do great business, straight up, as across-the-board professionals. The team has never forgotten a business associate who helped Melissa at some point in her career. They've not only kept track of everyone (no small feat), but have made it a habit to send us all greeting cards on special holidays—Christmas, Valentine's Day, St. Patty's Day, Easter. It's still a thrill for me to receive these charming hand-signed cards, and you can bet I listen to Melissa's new singles first when they come into the office!

Melissa and her teammates work hard, which is why she has had 12 consecutive Grammy nominations (as of 2003). Whether she's hosting a national event or at the top of the charts, she's undeniably unique and true to herself. There is only one Melissa. Bravo!

Make a Plan

Introduction: Planning Is the "Godmother" of Creativity

The difference between a musician who makes it and one who doesn't is simple. The successful one had a plan and followed it. It doesn't mean they followed the plan to a T, or that it necessarily led them down the path they originally envisioned. But they did have a plan and it did lead *somewhere!*

There is a popular misconception that planning "hampers" the spontaneity of creativity. Actually, making a plan is the *most* important activity you can undertake to support your creative efforts. It's a lot easier to "let it flow" when you know you have time set aside to write, an appropriate rehearsal space, the money for that new amp, and a series of shows to practice your chops. How can you relax enough to even begin to tap into your talent consciousness if you are worried about these other distractions?

Planning is the "godmother" of success, no matter how you define success for yourself. The most indie alternative band, the most badass rap group, the most pristine opera diva, and the biggest crossover country artist all started with a plan. A thoughtful plan will also go a long way to ensuring others treat your music seriously.

This chapter will walk you through a few simple steps that help you use your unique talents to make a well-rounded, realistic plan for achieving your artistic and business goals. We'll also talk about

Nadine Sez

My own mentoring story

When I moved to San Francisco in 1975, I was a huge Janis Joplin and Jefferson Airplane fan. I wanted to get into the San Francisco music scene and be around brilliant, creative people. I knew who Nick Gravenites was from reading album credits and rock articles. He had produced and written for Janis Joplin and Paul Butterfield, produced Brewer and Shipley, and started the seminal blues/rock/horn band, Electric Flag. Nick was a local star and often played around town in intimate clubs with Michael Bloomfield and Mark Naftalin.

I started going to Nick's gigs. I found out he played regularly at the (in)famous Saloon in North Beach. I started hanging out there looking for a chance to speak with him. When the opportunity presented itself, I took it! I was nervous and shy, but determined to eventually be recognized as cool and smart enough to be one of those SF people who made, supported, managed, and promoted music. A chance taken with a small conversation slowly turned into a deep friendship, and then a career. I had been afraid that my inexperience and business naïveté would be a deterrent, but I found that a shared loved of music was enough for Nick.

Later we found ways to help each other more concretely. I managed his day-to-day activities, booked his shows, and publicized his career, while he introduced me to business people and artists. I met members of the Grateful Dead family, singer Maria Muldaur, Paul Butterfield, John Cippolina of Quicksilver Messenger Service, and Rick Danko of the Band. I met blues harmonica great James Cotton and saw an the importance of partnerships, mentors, and why a budget is absolutely necessary, no matter how little money you might have to invest in yourself.

Success, Flexibility, and Accountability

Success is not something unattainable. Success is the immediate result of making a good decision. The template for success is the same, whether it's your local neighborhood club or a 1,000-seat

album Nick produced for Chicago blues guitarist Otis Rush get nominated for a Grammy Award.

Later Nick introduced me to Pete and Jeannette Sears. Pete played bass and keyboards in Jefferson Starship and we all became close personal friends. Nick also introduced me to the writer John Grissim, who in turn introduced me to Bill Thompson and Jacky Sarti, who both ran Jefferson Airplane/Starship. One introduction led to another, another, and yet another.

Nick embraced old and young musicians equally in his love of music.

He had brilliant young associates (my contemporaries) like the stunning guitarist Jimmy (Toast) Ralston and harmonica ace Huey Lewis, who would occasionally join him as sidemen at gigs, as well as established guitar legend John Cippolina. The only criterion was loving to play music live.

For those of us who were younger, it was inevitable that we all move on.

At the end of my tenure with Nick, I saw the Clash perform before Nick's band took the stage at a hippie revival festival in Monterey in 1979. It mirrored the dichotomies in my own life. I was anxious to spread my wings on a national level and get on with my success. The Searses arranged for me to take over a publicity position with Jefferson Starship. I started the day "Jane" was released as a single—October 15, 1979. Around the same time, Ralston moved to Los Angeles and found a job with Tina Turner. A short time later, Tina was rediscovered and her career relaunched by A&R legend Carter. Lewis started his own band, American Express, but changed the name to Huey Lewis and the News when American Express Corporation sued him for using the name. He got a savvy manager, Bob Brown, and then a record deal with Chrysalis. Yet another generation was on its way....

venue. Every step of the way, you simply integrate a more enhanced version of the same types of activities.

Success is made of up of very simple little things: writing a good song, having a productive rehearsal, making an effective demo, getting the right gig, writing an engaging press release, finding a talented producer. Stringing together simple successes gives you larger successes. Get in the habit of laying the groundwork of your success now, so when success really does come to you on the level you desire, you'll already be familiar with how the process works. Success will be second nature. And it won't be necessary for you to forget your priorities, divorce your wife, or become a junkie.

Flexibility in planning is key, since circumstances and criteria change. The goals that were attractive three years ago are either outdated or lack the same appeal they once had for you. If you force yourself to continue on a path you've come to abhor, you will stop creating and most often will take out your frustrations in inappropriate and destructive ways (like melting down at your biggest gig and walking off the stage).

Personal accountability is a private promise you make to yourself. Since things rarely happen in the business in any predictable manner, you are the one responsible for grounding yourself and keeping yourself grounded. This is your commitment to yourself. This is the discipline and hard work that success demands on any level.

Link Artistic and Business Goals

Many artists feel there is a dividing line between their art and commerce. After crafting their CDs with love and care, musicians stop thinking when the record is ready for release. They panic, wasting valuable time and resources. The same elements of talent that helped you make a great record will be the same elements that help you craft a great strategy. It would be disappointing for you to have the best songs and not have a good business plan to match their skill level.

Good business is as creative as a well-written song. Like a song, there is the constant daily repetition of the chorus, which brands your identity. There is something unique in your presentation and ability to perform that gets others' attention. There is the bridge that connects the different elements of your talent to your audience, the media, and business agents. If you can collaborate with your drummer to arrange a song, you can collaborate with a club owner to book a show. If you can convince your lead guitar player why he can only solo for three minutes, you can convince that weekly newspaper to run your band's picture for the upcoming show.

Research and Assess Strategies

Study, read, and educate yourself on the way music business is done. Do your homework. Avail yourself to the myriad business plans that other bands, companies, and managers have used. There is no excuse in today's world for an artist to live in a vacuum, unless it's self-imposed. The books and Web sites in the "Further Reading" guide at the back of this book should help you.

Research who is doing business the way you want to do business. Talk to other artists to find out how they do business. Weekly newspapers, music magazines, and online communities offer a wealth of information on how to reach other musicians. Read the local entertainment papers, listen to the local music shows, and monitor the "specialty" shows on the radio to see what other like-minded artists are doing. It's up to *you* to find the pieces of your own career puzzle, be they other bands, colleagues, writers, producers, or fans.

Making a feasible plan means having a realistic goal. Making your first demo in Joe's garage and then headlining RFK Stadium is not realistic. Making a demo in Joe's garage and then obtaining a local club date is realistic. Unrealistic plans are recipes for disaster because they encourage farfetched expectations, which lead to the frustrations that cause bands to break up. Achievable plans are not only encouraging, but they get you from step A to step B, move you forward, and give you a sense of accomplishment.

You sabotage yourself with unrealistic planning. Nothing is worse than a band insisting on showcasing to the industry before they are ready. Poor set list, inept stage presence, and a disposable demo situation could have been avoided by employing a realistic plan. The more practice you have making a plan, the easier it will become to regularly accomplish your goals. Make realistic planning a productive habit.

Discipline and Routine

Bands need to set higher standards for themselves. Get in the routine of being productive. The adage "success is 90 percent perspiration and 10 percent inspiration" is truer than you would like to think. Much creative time is spent on the mundane side of creation, working out chords, harmonies, and song structures *over* and *over* and *over* again. It's a lot like your school days of piano practice, but now you are practicing for yourself, not your folks and teacher! You should have a repertoire of at least ten songs before you are ready to spend time on gigs, set lists, travel logistics, and load-in duties.

Establish a Support System

If you and your band mates don't have the same goals, seriously reconsider whether you want to keep working with them. If you want to write pop songs, and your band mates are into heavy metal, quit wasting your time and look for musicians who have your same aspirations.

Bands break up because the criteria for band members change. It may be inevitable that you go your divergent directions. Musicians often start off in one genre of music but evolve into a different genre. That's artistic growth. You should not only accept such change but encourage it, so you can get down to who you really are.

Be with people who have the same value system. Values build an unshakeable foundation. When you are doing business with people who have like-minded values, you don't worry about lying, cheating, or stealing. Or, if this is how you prefer to do business, then at least you will know what your cohorts are up to and can protect yourself accordingly.

If you establish a drug-free environment now, it won't be so hard to maintain it down the line when success comes your way along with the subsequent temptations of fame. Or, if you like sex and drugs, you'll be well versed in how to spot those who will and those who won't.

Nadine Sez

The balance between art and commerce

*T*he balance between art and commerce lies between satisfying yourself and satisfying others. Artists get stubborn, draw a line, and don't want to compromise. Compromise gets a bad rap. It's knowing when and what to compromise that is the secret. Pick your battles wisely, using your knowledge of what is important to you and what is important to "them." "Them" can be anyone from a club owner to a manager to a label.

What's more important: recording on 64 tracks or having more money for touring? What's more important: having your name legible at the top of the CD, or your girlfriend's original artwork pristine on the cover? What's more important: having a 60-minute sound check or going on in the middle slot?

You decide. These are your choices. Decide according to your circumstances, desires, goals, and strategy. If you choose your girlfriend's pristine but ineffective cover artwork, be prepared to have people bypass it in the CD bin when they can't read your name.

When I counsel bands, I can usually tell who has a fighting chance and who doesn't. The ones who are immensely creative but clueless on how to present their talents are sad cases for me. Why spend all this time making the effort only to hamper the project by not having a plan? Poor commitment and poor accountability have sabotaged many a fine effort. If you find yourself blaming everyone else (the band, the club, the stupid fans, that awful radio station), then you may not be making the right person accountable: you.

Just because a music professional, label, or manager takes an interest, that doesn't mean you've arrived. Many bands expect something to *happen*, right away! "Interest" means: "Let's start a conversation, maybe we'll date a bit to see if we're compatible." It doesn't mean: "Howdy stranger, let's run off and get married!" When bands don't get the attention they desire from the industry, they blame the industry, instead of their own lack of talent or drive.

Let's face it. No matter how much you strategize and market, if it's not a hit, it's not a hit. You may be the nicest fellow in the world—but no chops, no songs, and no presence means no career.

A support system of your peers ensures support to carry you through the rough times. Your peers challenge you to create your best and collaborate with you on projects. No matter how much your wife/husband, girlfriend/boyfriend, Mom/Dad, and sister/brother love you, they do not understand what you are going through. They do not understand why you are compelled to such actions as driving all day just to record all night. No one understands what it's like wrestling with those creative and business demons except other people going through the same process.

Make Partnerships with Other Bands

Artists like other artists. If you like their music, there is a very good chance they will like your music. *Contact them!* Other bands can become colleagues in brainstorming, not to mention the sharing of rehearsal space, equipment, gigs, and contacts. You can also share information with these bands. While a manager may not be right for one band, he or she may be right for yours. An A&R resource may be looking at that other band's music and recognize your music warrants their attention.

If you want to be around certain types of people, find them! Since they don't know you, you must go to them. Find out how to reach them and *contact them.* If you like what someone else is achieving and you're doing something similar (not stylistically, necessarily, but with the same sensibilities), there is a very good chance that they will like what you're doing.

If you know a certain band is recording at a certain studio, think about booking yourself in there at the same time. If you know a band is playing a certain club, you should go down there when they are playing. You may not be able to get backstage to Pink or the Hives, but on the local level, you can certainly meet people that are on the same path and at the same shows.

Talk to other artists. Talking to each other about frustrations, fears, and strategies enables you to demystify the process of creativity for yourself, negate the frustrations, and make the successes more rewarding. It's your support system of peers that you turn to when you find yourself unable to write that song...or that hook won't come...or your bass player is late again...or you can't get the agent on the phone…or you just got the middle slot on Saturday night…or you got the side stage for Dave Matthews!

I've found that as bands work together and get friendly with other bands, they move up the "success" food chain in like fashion. Although their movements are different (different genres, different directions), they will all be moving ahead at about the same pace. First they get bigger shows, then better business connections, then greater success. I'm convinced it's because they goad, confide, comfort, challenge, and compete against one another.

Identify a Mentor

Every successful musician or music business person had someone already established in the profession take them under their wing. By

Nadine Sez

The industry is not a private club

One common misconception is that the music industry is a type of secret club, closed to outsiders, making it impossible to break into "the business." This simply isn't true. What is true is the fact that the business is too crowded with records and output. Sheer necessity demands a screening process. No one has the time to wade through the myriad of calls and product to see who is and isn't legitimate.

In this business, you're judged only by success. Success is defined only by record or ticket sales. This seems so daunting to rookies, neophytes, and outsiders that they often give up before they can gain a solid foothold. Don't forget the business is *always* looking for the next success. Determining your goals, making a good plan, sticking with it, and aligning yourself with like-minded people will all go a long way to getting you into the rhythm of the business.

Familiarity plays a big part in industry recognition. Once people see you are serious about matters at hand—talking the lingo and walking the path of commitment—they will be more willing to share information, give you strategic tips, and consider working with you.

listening to your questions and replying professionally, these mentors offer invaluable assistance to your career planning and business credibility.

Mentors see a spark of potential in you. This professional recognition may instill in you the confidence necessary to follow through on your goals. Mentors are sounding boards to help ensure your strategy is solid. They often can tell you the professional status or reputation of those you might be contacting. Their encouragement and experienced wisdom are invaluable. Mentors rarely get you a deal, assist you in business, or become your manager. Rather they prevent you from making costly mistakes (in terms of time, reputation, or actual expense) when you don't know what you are doing in business dealings.

If you are serious about your music career, find a mentor. Go to industry shows and conferences, music festivals, recording studios, and industry business events (such as celebrity charity golf or bowling). Read the music industry trade magazines and Web sites. If you connect with a mentor, I guarantee something good is happening in your music. Either your songs are beginning to gel, your stage show is finally coming together, or you've finally developed an identifiable band sound. If you are a business person, then your band's music has developed enough to get someone's real attention.

However, just because you want a mentor is no guarantee you will find one. No one in the business has any time to waste on people who are not serious, so unless you work hard on your development, you may not hit the criteria necessary to be taken seriously.

Begin a Budget

No matter how small a budget you have, you must have one. Good budgeting alleviates headaches, whether you have $200, $2,000, or $20,000. Alleviating headaches alleviates frustration. Knowing how much money you need for your project will determine whether you finish recording, go on tour, or make a poster for the gig.

Decide how much money you need, and then how to get that

money. Spend it wisely, keeping your end goal in mind. Money has a way of coming to people who are very specific about their needs. Actually sitting down with pencil in hand to plan your budget can be as good as writing a hit song since it won't do you any good to write that song if you don't have the money to record it! It's frustrating if you can't afford to fix the van when it breaks down or replace the amp when it blows up. Equally frustrating is when you've got 1,000 CDs sitting in Mom and Dad's garage because you don't have any money left to hire anyone to promote or publicize the recording.

Get into the habit of fiscal responsibility now, while the money is small. This will make the difference when you get $20,000 from an indie label to make an EP, or $300,000 from a major to make a full-length CD, or $2,000,000 for a TV special. Because of your prior experience with *routine* fiscal responsibility you will know how to budget effectively and responsibly, regardless of the dollar figure. Don't sabotage yourself. It's your money. Don't throw that money away. Create good fiscal habits by making specific budgets.

There are plenty of guidelines out there for routine budgeting, but this *is* the music business after all, so be sure to remember to plan for contingencies. Pad your budgets, because your costs are always about 25 percent more than what you anticipate. If there is more than a 25 percent differential between what you planned and the actual costs, generally there's something wrong with your expenses or your figures.

Chapter 2 Keywords

1. **Planning** is the bedrock of success.
2. Make **appropriate** choices.
3. Get into a **routine**.
4. Create **partnerships**.
5. Write a **budget**.

Once you have prioritized your efforts, you can sit down and make a time line to implement your plan!

REAL-WORLD SUCCESS STORY

Guitarist Craig Chaquico

One artist I've worked with closely who had to assess his plan to see if it was feasible was guitar great Craig Chaquico. Craig was a Sacramento, CA, high-school student when he was discovered by Paul Kantner and Grace Slick playing in a club band (complete with fake mustache to look older). After playing on their solo projects, he was asked to join their new post-Jefferson Airplane band, Jefferson Starship. As the boy wunderkind, he was young, good-looking, and phenomenally talented on guitar.

This new '70s reincarnation of one of America's favorite bands took off with the hit "Miracles." Craig went from high-school club gigs to stadium shows, private jets, and multimillion album sales. Despite new lineups (Marty Balin, Grace Slick, Johnny Barbata left, Mickey Thomas and Aynsley Dunbar joined, Grace came back, Paul left, etc., etc.) and name changes (Starship), this success continued well into the '80s (three No. 1 radio hits in '84, '85, and '86) before the last vestiges of the band called it a day and sputtered to a close in 1990.

At that point Craig was anxious to continue playing. He had always felt somewhat overlooked in the guitar realm and felt he had a lot of life left in his career. He put together a hard-rock outfit called Big Bad Wolf, complete with a good-looking rock singer, long hair, and power chords (imagine some variation of Warrant). They started showcasing for labels.

The problem was that it was 1991 and the rage was Seattle grunge music. Big hair was out, power chords were out, and '80s rock bands were out. Despite months of showcasing, and the push of respected management, record labels weren't interested and Craig started to get discouraged.

It was around this time that we talked. I had already been producing BMI showcases in Portland, Seattle, and San Francisco, and I knew firsthand how quickly music and audiences were changing. I asked Craig if he had anything else he was working on and he said he was playing around in his studio with some acoustic stuff. I asked him to send it to me.

When I received it, I was knocked out! He had always been a good songwriter for the two Starships, but his fantastic sense of melody now took center stage. His guitar playing, unfettered by the constraints of a rock band and enhanced by the clarity of the acoustic sound, soared. Wow!

I had discovered a new age label called Higher Octave through my friend Rena Shulsky and immediately thought of them. They were just then losing their marquee act, Ottmar Liebert, whose contract was up, and I knew they would need a high-profile artist to keep their momentum going. New age was a brand-new music genre at the time, best known for hippie-world-soft-jazz music and a loyal audience. It was quickly becoming a more sophisticated medium and I thought Craig could get in on the ground floor and write his own ticket.

I called my friends at Higher Octave, Dan Selene and Matt Marshall, and then sent them a tape of Craig's acoustic work. Craig had never intended to shop these as demos. He was just exploring some new musical paths and noodling around. But as I expected, the Higher Octave folks liked them.

Of course, I also did a strong sell on Craig to the label. Having worked with him for ten years, I knew his strengths beyond his guitar playing. A gifted raconteur, he was an excellent radio interviewee, had a great knack for developing a quick rapport with an audience, and understood the promotional aspects of the music business. Plus he was already a well-known entity in the rock radio world—no small feat.

Unfortunately, Higher Octave was still new to the mainstream music business and didn't understand the value of Craig's entertainment acumen in addition to his musical talents. And Craig still considered himself a rock guitar star. He had never seriously considered a career in this decidedly unrock new genre—he was just playing around. He had never heard of Higher Octave Records. The money certainly wasn't in the rock star range. And let's face it, Eddie Van Halen wasn't making new age records.

I made Craig and keyboard partner Ozzie Ahlers come into my office. They sat on the couch and told me that their manager could get them a rock band deal with a big time record mogul, Irving Azoff, who once had been a major force in the music industry.

I told them that Azoff could give them a deal but the record wouldn't sell or be promoted because he only had a "boutique label" with a major label, and the majors promote their own acts first. More time would go by while Craig got yanked around by the conglomerate, taking him further and further away from the public eye. I told them rock bands were dead and no one cared if he had been in Jefferson Starship (no offense to anyone). In fact, no one cared about Irving Azoff anymore either.

I pointed out that these guys at Higher Octave were hungry and wanted to score with their label. Craig would get *all* their attention. The entire focus of their company would be on selling his record. They were not married to prescribed marketing strategies and might think more outside the box.

I also pointed out that this was a new medium he could grow along with as the audience grew. Did he really want to be playing in rock bands for another 20 years? He was still a young guy, having started as a high schooler, but none of us can be 20 forever.

This was a tough conversation for many reasons, not the least of which was my honesty about the business and Craig's place in it, if he continued on the rock path. I didn't have anything better to offer him except my faith in this new opportunity with Higher Octave. Faith. But no matter what I thought, this was Craig's and his family's livelihood. He was a known entity as a rock god. Why would anyone mess with that?

After much introspection, Craig did go on to sign with Higher Octave. He is now one of the preeminent smooth jazz artists in the country. He is a Grammy Award nominee, saw his album *Acoustic Planet* go to No. 1 on the *Billboard* New Age charts, and had smash No. 1 and No. 2 radio hits with "Luminosa" and "Cafe Carnival." In 2003, his catalog surpassed one million units shipped. Craig has actually influenced the sound you hear today on smooth jazz radio, incorporating the best elements of rock guitar playing into this melodic format. When you go to see Craig live, he still does all the guitar god tricks (playing with his teeth, playing behind his head) you've come to know and love.

Backstage with Primus bass player Les Claypool, guitar ace Craig Chaquico, and sax man Clarence Clemons at the Bay Area Music Awards, 1991. Craig has created opportunities for himself because he remains open to new possibilities.

I admire him greatly for his realistic career evaluation post-Starship. Because he was open to new creative opportunities, and willing to work hard, he's been able to redefine his success by creating new partnerships and attracting new audiences. His achievements should be inspiring to all of us who face these same career challenges.

Craig is unique. Not many musicians have had the success in even one career that he has had in two…and he's still going strong! Fantastic!

REAL-WORLD SUCCESS STORY:

Manager Gary Falcon

I was first mentored by Nick Gravenites of Electric Flag and Janis Joplin fame. Jacky Sarti (former wife of Peter Kaukonen, Jorma's brother), who was the longtime office manager—and glue—of the Jefferson Airplane/Starship corporation, later took me under her wing. Other mentoring stories include Bonnie Simmons, longtime industry professional, manager, and radio personality, who mentored Adam Duritz from Counting Crows (after I had given her some early demos). Eric Godtland, manager of Third Eye Blind, mentored Tim O'Brien when he was managing the young, up-and-coming band Stroke 9. Highly regarded Los Angeles attorney Kim Guggenheim mentored Smash Mouth manager Robert Hayes. And so it goes….

My favorite mentoring story, however, concerns the irrepressible Gary Falcon, now president of Falcon-Goodman Management and responsible for the careers of country acts Travis Tritt, JEB, and Christy Sutherland. Over a game of eight ball at a saloon in San Francisco's Haight-Ashbury began one of my most enduring personal and professional friendships.

In 1984 I was a guest lecturer in the SF State University music industry program. As director of promotion and publicity for Jefferson Starship, I tried to give these bright and inquisitive kids a realistic view of the music biz. One night, after leaving work at the Airplane Mansion, I was shooting pool in one of the local hangouts on Haight Street. The club manager, a kid named Gary Falcon, came up and introduced himself to me. He had a bit of experience working with some one-hit rock acts but was looking to move up into a better job with a management company. After hearing me speak at SF State he wondered if he could work for me. I told him I had no budget for an assistant at that time. Undeterred, he asked if he could intern for me. I said it would have to be for free and he said that would be fine, he just wanted the experience.

Although I gave him the menial, arduous office tasks no one likes, he never complained. Instead Gary used every opportunity to watch, listen, and learn. He was so determined to succeed he actually juggled working at a large insurance company from 6:00 A.M. to 10:00 A.M. before taking the bus to my office to work from noon until 6:00 P.M., after which he would go to his club gig. It didn't take a rocket scientist to see right away that this guy had everything on the ball. He was hip, reliable, smart, determined, and *self-motivated.* He wanted to learn as much as he could about the music business and he was passionate in his approach—all the benchmarks necessary for success. He simply needed more hands-on experience.

Gary became a valuable asset to me and after several months I wrangled a small but manageable weekly stipend for him, as he became my full-time assistant. Later, when his hours had to be cut due to a band hiatus, I helped him get a part-time job with another local management company so he could pay his bills. He worked for me for about three years before he decided to move to Nashville. He needed more responsibility and challenges than I could give him.

San Francisco, then as now, was pretty much a Mom-and-Pop music business town and there wasn't much chance for advancement for him. He thought Nashville might provide greater opportunity for him to become a manager, his life-long dream.

Moving lock, stock, and barrel to Nashville, he found full-time employment as the tour manager for a country duo, Sweethearts of the Rodeo, for two and a half years. While it provided the valuable experience he so desperately needed, it was not enough to support him financially or mentally. One day he called me, deeply depressed about his future. He didn't think his career was going anywhere and he was dejected. He had an opportunity to go on the road with Ricky Van Shelton but was ready to call it quits.

Corny as it sounds, I gave him the old pep talk. I truly felt that with all his talent and drive, success was just around the corner for him. I encouraged him to stay the course and give it a few more months. Shortly thereafter, mega-manager Ken Kragen gave Gary the break he was looking for: management rep and point person for Travis Tritt. Within two years, Gary had become a management partner with Ken. Travis later took Gary on as his sole personal manager. Falcon-Goodman Management was responsible for Travis's great comeback in 2001 and 2002. Gary's roster currently has Tritt and two new Sony artists soon to be hugely famous, JEB and Christy Sutherland. No one could be prouder than me about Gary's success (except maybe his folks and his daughter, Lena)! I'm sure he's now mentoring someone else along, just as I mentored him.

Write a Time Line

Introduction: Everyone Needs a Map

Everyone needs a map to the gold. Everyone is clueless in the beginning. Every superstar started at the bottom and worked their way up through hard work and commitment. No matter who it is, from that pierced and tattooed metal monster to that tall, reedy singer-songwriter, they each had to follow a series of steps to gain greater and more widespread attention.

This chapter will review the basics that go into writing a time line, especially the three-month rule.

Time Line Basics

A time line is a concrete visualization of what you are actually going to do in the next month, three months, six months, and one year. Time lines are designed to map out careers in a flexible fashion, with room for adjustments and changes when necessary. Your time line changes to match how your art and career change.

How can you know what you are going to do in the next month, the next three months, the next six months, the next year? Decide what you want to achieve and work backwards, breaking it down into small but effective activities.

Three-month increments are good for three reasons:

1. They give you a chance to *create achievable results.*
2. *You won't wander too far off the beaten path,* in case you have to make course corrections.
3. Most people *can't envision beyond* three months.

In three months you can put a band together…write three songs…record a working demo to send to clubs. In the next six months you can gig at out-of-the-way places on bad nights to get your set together…get a small fan base going…work the Internet. Three months after that you can be playing opening slots on weekends…building your crowd…doing better publicity…getting your name around…creating a buzz. In one year's time, you could be playing on a sold-out Saturday night.

If you want a big name producer, you would time line back the steps necessary—or work backwards from your end goal—to attract their attention. This would include writing an attention-getting song. This song would be good enough to get a local producer of note to record it. This recording would be good enough to get played on a local demo or specialty show. This airplay would catch someone's ear who could recommend it to a better-known producer.

The following general time line is designed to show what might be appropriate for most beginning bands who have big aspirations. Every activity in this time line is dealt with in more detail in later chapters. This example is just *one way* you might approach your career.

General Time Line Example

Year One Goal: Put a band together

Months 1–3:

- See lots of bands perform in music clubs.
- Post flyers in rehearsal spaces, guitar stores, coffeehouses, and recording studios.
- Place ads in newspapers, music newsletters, and on Internet music sites.

Months 4–6:

- Start to play and write songs with people who have responded to your ads.
- Discard apparent flakes, crazies, losers, psychos, and drama queens.
- Finalize solid lineup of flakes, crazies, losers, psychos, and drama queens masquerading as solid players.
- Start to write and play together.
- Start to get an image of you as a band.
- Let your daydreams run wild.
- Record bad rehearsal sessions and have fun.

Stay on track

*A*lthough I keep insisting you have to be flexible, unless opportunity presents itself, *do not* change your plan in midstream. If you're like me, you panic because things are not happening as quickly as you want. You begin to have self-doubt and to second-guess yourself.

If you've really sat down and taken the time to devise a good strategy, then give yourself time to allow it to take effect. Because of the nature of the business, some things are impossible to accomplish in a short period of time. For example, you must tour a market at least three times to even hope to begin to develop a fan base. Don't give up, just because you get impatient.

Months 7–9:
- Get more comfortable and confident playing music as you realize no one will laugh at you.
- Begin to meet other bands more confidently.
- Commit to a serious rehearsal schedule.
- Realize that band members come and go as things get more serious.
- Invest in some better equipment.
- Develop the beginning of a 45-minute set.

Months 10–12:
- Play low-key shows in nontraditional venues and small clubs, or on off-nights in larger clubs.
- Understand that a nontraditional venue may not present live music currently but will consider your proposal.
- Remember that audiences in small neighborhood clubs are generally friendlier and less demanding than showcase clubs.
- Realize that showcase clubs may be open to you playing on an off-night just to see how many people you can pull in.

Year Two Goal: Headline a major club on a weekend night
Months 1–3:
- Put shows together with other bands.
- Create a Web page with basic info: name, picture, gig schedule.
- Begin to create an Internet fan base with e-mail lists.
- Work on building a solid set list of songs.

Months 4–6:
- Record a decent three-song demo using a basic digital audio workstation, or rent an inexpensive digital studio.
- Play more visible shows with increasing attendance.
- Tighten up the pacing of the show and eliminate long breaks between songs and equipment changeovers.
- Engage in more aggressive street marketing to increase your recognition factor with the general public in your area.

Months 7–9:
- Get demo reviewed in local papers and fanzines.
- Get demo reviewed on Internet music sites.

- Put good reviews on Web site.
- Put MP3 of demo songs on Web site.
- Get demo played on a local college radio show.
- Get on weekend shows in opening or middle slot.

Months 10–12:
- Develop an attractive bill of solid bands with consistent draw of fans.
- Give the bill a name/theme/tag line, such as White Punks on Dope, Heavy Metal Blowout, Hot Country Nights, Songbirds Unplugged, Rocking Night of the Year, or Blues Jam Explosion.
- Sell lineup to a local club for a weekend night appearance.
- Make yourself the headliner.
- Use college radio to promote your big weekend show by giving away tickets over the air.
- Advertise your show with flyers and postcards.
- Decide what makes this show special, concentrating on attention-getting facts: rare occasion to see a certain band; special guests; reputations of the other bands including sold-out shows or better-than-average record sales; drink specials; ticket discounts for fans who meet certain criteria (arriving early, sisters who show I.D., or men dressed as Deborah Harry).
- Use special aspects of the show to interest the press in mentioning it as a noteworthy, exciting entertainment event.
- Highlight the show on your Web site and give tickets away via the site.
- E-mail your fan list and give tickets away via e-mail.
- Headline your weekend show and sell out, having to turn fans away at the door.

Year Three, Goal A: Record a CD with a professional producer
Months 1–3:
- Ask your band friends for producer recommendations.
- Look on the back of your favorite CDs for studios, producers, and engineers who have worked with bands in your area.
- Pick five in each category of producers, engineers, studios.
- Contact these people (if you contact 15 people, you will most

likely hear back from five, and one to three of them will be interested in working with you).

Months 4–6:

- Record a CD (or EP) with one of the contacts who responded favorably.

Year Three, Goal B: Sell your recording independently

Months 7–9:

- Release the CD by placing it on consignment in local music stores.
- Post it for sale on your Web site and online music sites so you can track your sales and fan interest.
- Get the CD reviewed in your local press, fanzines, and Webzines to coincide with its release.
- Play a CD release party—big show that coincides with release, with attendant publicity and focus on the CD's availability.
- Get one cut played in regular rotation on your local college station (this means writing and recording one really good song that gets consistent reaction no matter who is listening— girlfriend, producer, club manager, or other band).

Months 10–12:

- Play area gigs regularly in and around towns within an evening's drive, selling the CD at shows.
- Put the CD in local music stores in each gig location.
- Perform live at record stores to promote CD sales—these are called "in-stores." (While many people think brick-and-mortar record stores are a thing of the past, they remain the most important link for building a fan base and getting exposure. Record stores—especially the independents—are the new town halls of music and should be used as fully as possible.)
- Continue to promote and sell on your Web site.
- Coordinate with each college radio station in each college town to help promote your show; offer to give away tickets or the CD so they can announce when and where you are performing and which record stores carry the disc.
- E-mail your fan list to call these stations and request a specific song from the record; call the music director every week and

tell him or her more and more good news about people's reactions to that specific song (press, sales, etc.).

- Get song added to play list of college station.
- Publicize this fact in your press releases and on your Web site.

Year Four Goal: Sign with an indie label
Months 1–3:

- Expand your scope regionally, picking another three towns to conquer, so your reach has a ripple effect through a region.
- Use the same steps, local music stores, college radio, the power of the Web.
- Keep Web site very current with up-to-date gig, radio, and

Affect your competition

*T*oday your competition is not with other bands but for someone's attention. Before anyone can spend their entertainment dollars, you must first get their attention. DVDs, videos, movies, video games, meals, travel, theater, cell phones, pagers, palm pilots, the Internet, and e-mail are just a few of the other distractions you are up against today.

Once you hook them, you can't waste any time explaining your songs. Every action you take should compel the listener to react to your music in a specific manner. Your music should induce them to go to your Web site, go to a live show, call a radio station to request a song, or go to a record store to buy the CD.

To increase the effectiveness of your efforts, try to include combining a live show with both radio activity and retail action for a more cohesive effort. College stations love ticket giveaways and local independent music stores are more open to local band marketing. You have to make an effort anyway to promote your show. Why not make the most effective use of your time by using your live performance as the crux of your efforts and calling local college radio and independent record stores with co-promotional opportunities?

press info: names of stations playing the CD, pull quotes from good reviews, fan response.

- Create a sense of happening around your endeavors—airplay, shows, and reviews—so people feel they can't miss one of your gigs (if you treat your show as just another ho-hum gig, so will your fans).
- Track your CD sales and emphasize them (if they are good) on your site and in your press releases.
- When you reach 1,000 in sales, throw a party—that's a big accomplishment and should get you some attention!

Months 4–6:

- Research indie labels by examining CD covers, browsing record stores, talking to your friends and other bands and club bookers, reading music magazines, and surfing the Internet.
- Find like-minded labels who are doing business the way you are doing business; pick 15 of them.
- Contact those labels and ask how they accept submissions.
- Contact managers who deal with those labels.
- Contact producers who deal with those labels.
- Contact other artists on those labels.
- Gather the facts about why you are right for that signing: record sales of 1,000 or more, proven fan base, regional touring experience, college airplay, and good press (all evidence that your music gets noticed and you are serious about your career).

Months 7–9:

- Sign deal with indie label.
- Make new record with that label.

Months 10–12:

- Strategize a one-year marketing plan with your label (that is about the life span of an indie record).
- Make sure the record is "set up" before release through coordination with record stores, artwork, radio stations, advertising, marketing.
- Think regionally first, and don't waste money on a national campaign that will spread your resources too thin.
- Think outside the box.

Year Five Goal: Sell over 10,000 indie records
Months 1–3:
- Employ traditional and nontraditional marketing tools like the Internet, late-night TV spots, neighborhood direct mail, trade magazines, fanzines, touring opportunities, sponsorships, and other creative tie-ins to market your record.
- Know what you want to achieve every month for the next year and set monthly goals to help you stay focused.
- Consider using industry events (radio softball games for charity or local awards shows) or college activities (free concerts, dorm parties) as focal points of high-profile activity.
- Use the year to build momentum, like a set list that is well paced—don't forget the ripple effect of activity.
- Create a big picture that audiences want to be a part of, using sustainable, dynamic, talked-about shows, visible record sales, and consistent music presence.

Months 4–12:
- Implement these strategies wisely, always making sure one activity leads to the next, and revamp strategies that are not effective. (Example: if your label has limited distribution, resist paying for radio promotion in regions that don't carry your record. Instead, concentrate on performing and selling your record where you are getting airplay and there are clubs to support you.)
- Tour regionally three times to make a noticeable impact (go into the market regularly—every three months).
- Use independent record stores, in-stores performances, promotional giveaways, college radio stations, fanzines, the press, the Web, and your fan base in every market to keep the momentum going.
- Engage people with your marketing campaign and compel them to buy the record, call the radio station, go to the Web site, and see you perform live.
- Give the people want they want: to have fun at live shows, to be part of a happening scene, and to hear something they can't find on TV, radio, or the Internet.

- Create touring scenarios with other genre-specific bands to co-promote your tours and share the promotional efforts.

Year Six Goal: Sign with a major label
Months 1–3:
- Use the authentic success of your recent year-long campaign to secure the services of a "name" producer.

Months 4–6:
- Record demo with three to five songs including one to three radio-friendly songs (songs that people feel commercial radio would play on the air in continual rotation); have three to five more songs waiting in the wings that have "radio" potential.

Months 7–9:
- Using the punch of your past success and your new producer, secure the services of a manager or an attorney to represent you to labels.
- Have one or the other actively shop the produced record.
- Prepare shows to give labels an opportunity to see you in settings you control—with your fans.
- Have past radio airplay and record sales stats available and substantiated.

Months 10–12:
- Knock 'em dead with blistering showcases.
- Get the deal!

Year Seven Goal: Record an album with a major label
Months 1–3:
- Buy drinks for all your friends to celebrate.
- Daydream about fast cars and MTV success.
- Look for producers and write songs.
- Hire a business manager to help budget your money, pay your taxes, and buy insurance.

Months 4–6:
- Get to know your label personnel.
- Start collaborating with them on the dimensions and follow-through of your project.
- Discuss other producers and studios.

- Have more budget discussions.
- Write more songs.
- Fret about the time it takes to work with a major label.
- Start preproduction, finally.

Months 7–9:
- Fall into despair about the slowness of a major label.
- Devise strategies to deal with your frustration and don't give your power away by letting the label take care of things.
- Keep playing and writing, focusing on potentially commercial songs.
- Search out new collaborations to keep challenging yourself.
- Experiment in your home with new sounds and new equipment to stay fresh.
- Demo your new songs on your desktop recording setup.
- Handle a lot of preproduction chores in your home studio.

Months 10–12:
- Record the "major-label record" with the producer and label as collaborators.
- Do overdubs and mixing.

Year Eight Goal: Release an album on a major label

Months 1–3:
- Continue working on overdubs.
- Work on CD artwork and credits.
- Begin planning CD release strategy—first single to be released and radio set up.

Months 4–6:
- Take new promo photos; plan image of the band.
- Record "can't miss" hit song at the eleventh hour.
- Have discussion with label regarding marketing strategy, touring possibilities, and CD rollout by the different label departments.
- Put record on hold while new promotion head takes over.

Months 7–9:
- Wait while mastering and manufacturing is completed.
- Monitor single's release 6 to 12 weeks before album's release.
- Participate in promotional campaign to major market radio stations and record stores in support of the first single.

- Appear at industry conventions, trade shows, and company meetings.

Months 10–12:
- Celebrate: Record released!!

Monitor your plan for effectiveness

It doesn't do any good to make a time line if you do not monitor it for effectiveness. If something is not working, face the fact that you may have to change your strategy, band members, or sound. Although it may be unpleasant, it may be your only option if you are serious about what you want to achieve.

Since this is a relationship-based business, personnel changes can be particularly difficult. Everyone thinks it's a joke when you say, "It's nothing personal, it's just business." But more often than not,

Nadine Sez

Warren Buffett marketing and flexibility

Warren Buffett, the financier, recommends buying only stocks whose products you actually use and understand. Ask yourself how you, as a consumer, buy or go to see music. Market your music in the same way. Trying to market yourself in a fashion that is unfamiliar or foreign to you doesn't work.

Creative business flexibility is also key when you must make changes in your activities. Quicksilver Messenger Service and Melissa Etheridge both dumped their first records and re-recorded them. Stroke 9 remixed a good half of their first record after it had already gone to master. Smash Mouth canceled a tour with Robbie Williams when the label wouldn't come up with tour support. Jefferson Starship brought in Mickey Thomas to replace both Grace Slick and Marty Balin, then brought Slick back, then changed drummers from Aynsley Dunbar to Donny Baldwin, then fired Paul Kantner, then lost David Frieberg and Pete Sears, and then had three consecutive No. 1 singles. The artist E went from a solo artist to the Eels. Part of early Third Eye Blind became Snake River Conspiracy. These are all examples of how bands have had to remain flexible to keep progressing forward.

it's true. Creating a plan is one thing, putting the team together to execute it is another.

Accountability must be included in your time line so problems are assessed and dealt with immediately as they arise. If the bass player keeps neglecting his flyer duties, maybe he is not as dedicated as you and is dragging you down. If the guitar player has a drug problem, acknowledging the situation will help you assess the problem and choose a solution.

Decide what things *must* happen before you can headline that club on a Saturday night! If the booker will not return your calls, maybe your draw is not substantial enough for that club and your headlining ambitions need more time to develop.

Continue to monitor the plan so it's moving you closer to your goals while reflecting your current situation. A business plan for music is different than a business plan to sell shoes. *Hits, fads,* and *opportunities* come and go more quickly than the norm. You need to be realistic about the changeable nature of things.

This is a wacky business, life is wacky, and anything can happen. The rehearsal studio can close down, your car can break down, a band member may lose a day job, move away, or get sick. If you start as a heavy-metal band and somehow end up indie acoustic, then the plan you made will need readjustment. You cannot send a folk song to hard-rock stations.

Flexibility is key. If you get offered a short tour with a national headliner but you were planning on recording during that time period, reassess the benefits of both. Be prepared to jump on the bandwagon when it arrives. This is a very quick-moving business, and you don't want to be left behind!

Chapter 3 Keywords

1. Be **flexible** but stay the course and let things develop.
2. Assign duties and plan activities in **three-month** increments.
3. **Work backwards** from your end goal to where you are today.

After sitting down with a time line, the time for pencil and paper is over. It's time to just start playing. At some point, you are going to want to step out of the rehearsal hall and see if an audience reacts to what you've been practicing. The next chapter talks shop about performing live.

REAL-WORLD SUCCESS STORY:

Grammy Award–Winning Train

Train is a good example of a band who performed live long enough to develop their own distinctive sound. Jimmy Stafford, Charlie Colin, and Rob Hotchkiss had all played in a band called the Apostles in Los Angeles. Rob met Pat Monahan and both moved north to San Francisco to pursue music. After Jimmy and Charlie joined them, they added Scott Underwood on drums, completing the nucleus of Train. This was around 1994, and shortly thereafter the band came to the attention of Bill Graham Management and signed a management contract.

While the band concentrated on building their fan base in the Bay Area, Bill Graham Management had them open several shows at San Francisco's legendary Fillmore. Although personable and obviously talented, they had yet to find their own band niche. Despite several industry showcases in 1996, including one I produced for BMI, no suitable record label offers were forthcoming. Even Sony Records, their future label, passed on the band at this time, following a New York showcase. The band and management had to reassess their strategies.

With funding from family and friends, Train released a CD on the Bill Graham Management label, Wolfgang Records. The recording came to the attention of Aware Records, a small Chicago label that had served as a developmental stepping stone for Matchbox Twenty and Better Than Ezra. Aware placed "Meet Virginia" from the Wolfgang CD on one of their hip compilations, *Aware 5*. Train then toured relentlessly back and forth across the US, polishing their sound and delivery while selling records. The catchy song caught the ears of programmers and things snowballed from there. At that point, Aware re-released the original CD and Sony stepped in to assist in radio promotion and video, and the single went on to became a VH-1 and radio hit nationwide.

Those years of constant touring really helped Train come into their own, musically and professionally. The band that left San Francisco on tour was not the one that returned to work with famed producer Brendan O'Brien. That relentless touring laid the mental groundwork for their sophomore multiplatinum smash "Drops of Jupiter" on Sony. Coming full circle from being dismissed as Counting Crows "wannabes," the band developed their own unique, appealing sound, now known throughout America simply as Train. Their current CD, "My Private Nation," continues with their highly identifiable, signature sound.

The band Train, along with Bill Graham Management staffers and BMI's Rick Riccobono, hanging backstage at my BMI showcase at Slim's nightclub in San Francisco, mid '90s. Constant touring kept Train on track to a successful sound and identity.

REAL-WORLD SUCCESS STORY:

Universal Recording Artists Stroke 9

Stroke 9's three original members met in a high-school class actually titled "How to Be in a Rock Band." From those auspicious beginnings they recruited a drummer friend and started Stroke 9. They remained committed through college and, after graduating, decided to pursue a major-label recording deal full-time. They started making demos and playing clubs, dives, frat parties, beach towns, colleges, and football games up and down the coast of California.

Their early performances attracted the attention of a fan, Tim O'Brien, who was booking small shows and bands while attending Cal-Berkeley. Tim joined Stroke 9 as manager, and the band increased their gigs and made new demos. After college, Tim went to work for Bill Graham Presents, but not in management. Armed with his business degree, he worked his way up from a slub producing corporate parties to artist relations (working with touring acts like the Rolling Stones) before moving into amphitheater development. But in the environment of Bill Graham Presents, he watched, listened, and learned. Tim approached me about S/9 playing the BMI showcase with Train in early 1997 but I declined, thinking they weren't ready for the majors at that time.

Stroke 9 continued on the artist development path in determined fashion, changing drummers (which made a huge musical and credibility difference) and eventually putting out their own independent record, *Bumper to Bumper.* They bought an attention-getting old ambulance as their touring vehicle and contacted press in every market, showing a knack for working every angle. Their efforts paid off as they developed an unusually large fan base in several regional markets and sold 10,000 copies of their self-released debut.

In 1998, I was showcasing a collection of San Francisco bands at the Viper Room in Los Angeles for BMI. Stroke 9's agent at the time, Yavette Holts, called and pestered me to put them on the bill. They had made a new $15,000 demo I had yet to hear. After listening to her, talking to Tim, and hearing the record, I knew things were popping for them, so I put them in my best slot, playing first.

Possibly due to the talent lineup or possibly due to the free drinks, the club was packed to the rafters that night. There was a broad mix of Los Angeles music industry scenesters, including promotions and publicity people amongst the normal contingent of lawyers and A&R reps. Several attorneys were jockeying for position to represent S/9 and there was a healthy buzz in the room.

I'll never forget Luke Esterkyn's striking presence onstage that night. People were really seeing him and the band for the first time, and everything clicked. Their good looks combined with a great selection of potential hit songs made for a captivating performance. I knew they were on their way when two industry people not in A&R wanted to call their bosses (heads of labels) immediately about the band.

But it was really all those years of constant writing, playing, working, publicizing, and recording that gave Stroke 9 the confidence to handle that moment in the Viper Room. And that moment started a chain of events that culminated in their record deal with Cherry Entertainment/Universal Records a few months later. Spurred by the single "Little Black Backpack," their major label debut album went on to sell over 600,000 copies and enabled them to tour worldwide.

Play Your Music Live

Introduction: Why Bands Need to Perform Live

As producer of many BMI showcases in the '90s, I chose the talent, arranged the venue, spearheaded the industry outreach, helped with publicity, and produced the show. The bands included an early version of the Dandy Warhols (called the Beauty Stab), 4 Non Blondes (whom I paid no attention since I was high on another band, whose name I've long forgotten), Counting Crows, Candlebox, Third Eye Blind, Train, and Stroke 9, among others. Having supported and worked with them in their early days, I'd like point out the value that playing live had on many of their careers.

Counting Crows' unique sound and their strong management/ lawyer team is what caught everyone's attention on the initial demos. But they had been playing the club scene for years in various combinations of musicians. It was not until after the industry saw them play my showcase at San Francisco's I-Beam nightclub before the Gavin Radio Convention that the Crows received those 12-plus offers in a major-label bidding frenzy. The show wasn't particularly that great as far as pacing or seamlessness, but you knew you were watching something unique and special. Adam Duritz's delivery that evening was rough and his voice was not great due to a cold. But his electrifying, soulful edginess captivated everyone there.

I've seen Third Eye Blind play to packed houses at the Paradise Lounge (500 people) and also play to 50 people. They were most successful when they played their warehouse parties. Stephan Jenkins paid his dues as a card-carrying, club-playing local musician in San Francisco (much to his frustration, sometimes) until he found a different route to success. I always thought playing live was the proving ground for 3EB as Stephan tried out different combinations of musicians to find the right fit for his strong personality. When he found the right combination, he found success with his hit "Semi-Charmed Life."

Backstage with members of Stroke 9 and producer Jerry Harrison (Live, Talking Heads) at the legendary Fillmore during Nadine's Wild Weekend, 1999. Steady gigging helped Stroke 9 stoke a fan base before they ever showcased.

The musicians in Train had been playing in bands since the late '80s. Once considered highly derivative, they toured constantly, refining their sound and presence in the mid-'90s. By the time you saw the video for "Meet Virginia" on TV, they had become a highly competent, confident band. By the time they recorded "Drops of Jupiter," they had developed a very, very original sound.

Nadine Sez

Audience appeal and fan respect

*M*any bands today complain how difficult it is to get the general public out to shows. The reason often is that the performers are not being entertaining enough, or the event is not compelling enough. The competition for the entertainment dollar today is *fierce*. With so many alternative amusement streams, performing artists must offer the fans something they can't find in other venues.

A highly original and entertaining performance is one draw. Creating a social ambiance that feels special is another. Most people go to live music shows to be entertained, to socialize, or to be part of a scene. Are you hitting these marks with your shows? Or are you just another derivative band on another boring three- to four-band bill, going through the paces?

Artists speak to and for the fans. When you tell artists to build a fan base, you are telling them to speak out and touch other human beings with words, verse, and music. Fan reaction is a response to artists speaking to something larger than all of us (an emotion, a sentiment, a sense of being).

Everyone wants to be part of something bigger. Artists take the risk for the fans and speak the common truths, absurdities, and reflections of all our lives, whether it's love, angst, responsibility, or loss.

A true fan base is built on mutual respect. Artists don't know any more than their fans, but they are willing to take the risk of singing, performing, speaking. This is an *equal exchange* of emotion, power, and energy, however. Artists who don't respect their fans are depriving them of an integral, appealing part of the process of exchange.

Stroke 9 played up and down the West Coast at clubs, colleges, and frat parties for eight years before signing with a major label. It enabled them to build a fan base, continue to write new material, and solidify their sound. They weren't ready to showcase in 1995, but after three more years of performing and songwriting, they were ready in 1998. One reason S/9 got signed after their Viper Room show was that people reacted to them live (borne out by their phenomenal fan base).

For all performers, live stages are the beckoning canvas on which they test out new material, garner new fans, and find their true voice of expression. No matter how good those demo tapes are, most labels—indie or major—still want to see bands live, so you better be able to play and get an enthusiastic response. A clever demo tape may get the label's attention, but you better have the substance, drive, and direction—generally only discerned through playing live—to go the distance.

Here are some **Dos** and **Don'ts** on how to get started playing live. You start by contacting club bookers, then move on to contacting other bands, which may not only help you get gigs but provide a comfort zone. You can also produce your own shows or find alternative venues. *Promoting* your show is just as important as your performance in many cases, if you want to be asked back. Finally, reflect on your stage presence and delivery, along with your pacing and song selection. It's not as easy as it looks. But when it all comes together, there is *nothing* as fulfilling as a good live show.

How to Contact a Club

Do send a three-song demo that best describes your *live* sound to the booking agent or manager of whatever club/coffeehouse in which you wish to perform. Many bands make a meticulous album that sounds nothing like them live. Clubs want to hear your *live* sound because they are trying to figure out how to book you on appropriate bills. Recorded and live sound are not always in concert. (How many times have we heard tapes only to find out later that the band couldn't play?)

Do contact the club *only* during the hours specified. Most club bookers are overworked bar employees who moonlight as bookers. Nothing is more annoying to them than getting called to the phone by a rookie band while they are trying to run a sound check, open the bar, or assist a load-in. Follow club etiquette.

Do call every week *until* you get a response. That is the only way they will finally pay attention to you.

Do leave factual information on your messages. This will help your cause. (Simply stating, "We're great, man, and everyone loves us" isn't enough to sway a jaded, tired club booker.) Such factual information might include the following:

1. Other venues you have recently played or are confirmed to play
2. Numbers of people at your last show
3. What you will do to promote your show
4. A good press review or mention of radio activity
5. Insights on how your music could support certain headliners

Do suggest complete bills to the booker, since they often don't have the time or the inclination to formulate great shows until you've proven yourself. It's in your best interest to do the thinking for them.

By suggesting complete bills, you can determine the headliner and then use them to position your band. You can help your attendance by associating with more successful bands. You'll also be much more in control of your show. The more you can take your activities out of someone else's hands, the better chance you have to make things work in your favor.

Call Other Bands

Don't be afraid to call other bands to be on their shows. One good way to gain entrance into a new club is by riding another band's coattails. That way a club can get to know you with little risk because you're coming in under the auspices of their headliners.

Playing with other bands can also take the pressure off your act having to provide *all* the prepromotion, gear, attendance, and other miscellaneous hoopla associated with playing live. However, to get into a headlining band's good graces, you may have to offer to do a disproportionate portion of the gig work, until you've established a rapport and they know you are serious.

Mentally and emotionally, playing with a more established band or just your friends can help calm your preshow jitters because you're around a supportive cast. Never underestimate the power of having a comfort zone to enhance your performance.

Produce Your Own Shows

You can offer to buy out the club and produce your own show. While this generally is a more expensive proposition, it remains an extremely viable alternative if there is no other way to get into the club. An additional advantage to a club buy out is that you generally control the start times and set lengths for the entire evening, which can be immensely helpful when you need a specific showcase for labels or sponsors.

Don't rely on what you make at the door to cover your costs! Have the money you need to rent the gear, rent the hall, pay the headliner, pay the sound person, pay the lighting tech, pay the doorman, pay for preshow advertising—*all up front.* Unless that money is guaranteed, your show may be a losing proposition. Inevitably it will pour down rain, or the Strokes will play a secret show across the street, or your headliner will cancel—and your intake at the door will shrink (and may not cover your costs).

Bands will often rent a club to impress a manager or an A&R rep only to have those people not show up. Be sure why you are spending this money (to increase your fan base, create a buzz, control the setting). Do not let the appearance or nonappearance of the so-called industry determine whether you feel the show is a success or failure.

Create Alternative Venues

Don't think you must depend on the traditional path of club gigs, beginning with off-night opening slots and working your way up to weekend player. It can be a very long and very frustrating process. I've seen many bands attain success by creating their own scenes and a buzz through using alternative venues. Think outside the box and create situations you can control to your best advantage and benefit.

Don't be just another band in the "band ghetto" with your hand held out. Most often you must create your own advantages instead of relying on the business to find a slot for you. One way to stand apart from the crowd is by playing in a nontraditional or new venue. Be proactive by producing your own shows; renting a venue;

buying out a club; or creating your own space in a coffeehouse, warehouse, park, or college dorm.

The obvious advantages to offering shows at alternative times (brunch) on off-days (Mondays or Wednesdays) and providing support services specific to your audience (child care) are these:

- You control the setting. Pick small places you can pack.
- It's a great way to play your material and check the crowd reaction, helping you build an effective set.
- It gives you a great attention-getting hook when you are trying to get folks to take your call, come see you, or listen to your record.
- You avoid the crowded competition of conflicting entertainment events on traditional weekend schedules.

Do think *way* outside the box. Play in a mall or record store or church parking lot. Play at high schools during lunch. Play colleges for free, in the quadrangles. After checking with your local ordinances, play on the street at 2:00 A.M. after the bars close. Call a space not generally used for music. If you're underage, consider having your parents run the shows.

Don't be afraid to go off the beaten path and recognize the needs of your fan base. Consider putting on shows at different odd times and places that fit your crowd. Sunday afternoons, Sunday nights,

Nadine Sez

Dead admiration

One reason I admired the Grateful Dead (yes, I was a Deadhead in the '70s) was because they came up with the most incredible live-performance philosophy I've ever seen. They would never play the same show twice. That simple nugget of thinking, whether intentional or not, spawned a legion of fans who were attracted to their live performances specifically to see what they would play. This in turn spawned a huge economic venture of taping, sharing, and releasing tapes from certain shows. What an incredible philosophy to keep your fans interested and involved.

and off-nights, in cafes, coffee bars, diners, and frat houses—all these can serve as offbeat, attention-getting venues.

Don't limit yourself by thinking there is only one way. No one has the corner on creativity, good ideas, or new ideas. There are as many different ways to play live as there are bands, songs, musicians, radio stations, producers, and shows on MTV. "House" concerts (the latest rage for acoustic or semiacoustic performers), teen clubs, and church naves are only a few of the alternatives if you think outside the box.

Promote Your Shows

It's impossible to build a fan base or refine your act if you cannot establish an audience for your shows. No one has the time to always check on when and where you might be performing. Fans cannot go see you if they don't know you're playing. Preshow promotion is generally key to live success until you develop a presence dynamic enough to create word-of-mouth excitement.

Consider promoting your shows with the following activities:

1. **Event title:** Naming your shows and making them thematic is an easy way to brand the event—consistently fun, sold out, packed, happening, cool, underground, acoustic, rockin', electronic, or whatever.

2. **Radio spots:** If your show is large enough to warrant the expense, advertising during local music shows on big radio stations in your town may be effective. You could do this in conjunction with other bands on the bill to lower your costs and make the show a real event.

3. **Print ads:** You can also partner in newspaper ads to the same effect, with the added advantage of branding your band's name to a wider audience.

4. **Advance publicity:** Having a thematic event with multiple acts can be newsworthy. Send out a press release with a picture three weeks before the event to get an item (not a story) in your local newspapers, weeklies, and music monthlies. Ten days before the event, call and try to get publications to run the picture with a blurb about the show in the listing or music section.

5. **Flyers and posters:** These are invaluable for branding your

event and letting people know you are performing. Flyers and posters set the tone and image of the event. Many cities are cracking down on these items, however, in an effort to keep telephone and light poles cleaner. An alternative is to use the store windows of coffeehouses, bars, copy shops, clothing stores, record stores, music equipment stores, bookstores, and electronics stores.

6. **Postcard mailings:** Despite the trend away from snail mail, I feel it's imperative to keep these mailings up to date. Postcards are still appropriate because many fans (including myself) need a tangible reminder in hand. It's also another opportunity to imprint (or brand) your logo and band style upon their consciousness.

7. **E-mail:** E-mails to your fan base are good, but they're instantly disposable (which is why you continue to send postcards). Limit your e-mails to weekly, then two days before the event. Don't overdo them, as people will stop reading them. Consider making your e-mails interactive, so your fans get:
   • Free tickets if they answer a trivia question correctly.
   • Free CD if they bring three friends to the show.
   • Discounted admission if they respond before a specific time.

Whether we like it or not, the only way to keep live clubs is to keep clubs packed. Besides, nothing is more discouraging than playing to an empty house. Since your are constantly battling to get the attention of a society continually distracted by modern technologies, preshow promotion should be on the same priority as a good rehearsal.

Stage Presence and Delivery

When you play a live show, focus on your stage presence and delivery. No one expects you to be polished or perfect. What people look for, though, is your ability to reach that kid in the back of the bar drinking and hitting on that girl. When you can get him to put down his drink, quit hitting on that girl, and pay attention to you, *then* you've got something going on.

Your stage presence and delivery should reflect what makes you special. Think of who you are as a performer and incorporate that into your presentation. Your delivery is a direct reflection of your personality. Whatever makes you unique should be broadcast on that stage through your performance. Artists whose shows mirror their personalities include Tori Amos, Radiohead, Marilyn Manson, Elton John, Sting, Madonna, the Strokes, Beck, Neil Young, Missy Elliot, TLC, Eminem, and Iggy Pop.

Your songs demand the best from you. Don't let a haphazard performance distract from the songs or your playing. Practice your delivery and work on your audience rapport. We live in a visually demanding world where audiences are spoiled by music videos and video games. They have short attention spans and are used to information being delivered in 30-second sound bites. To counter this, you have to make your performance consistently interesting on *all levels, all the time.* Give your audience something they can't find on MTV, on the Internet, or in a video game.

Set Length and Song Order

A musical set should take the audience on a journey, like a book. Start big with an arresting song and end with the same. In between, keep the pacing of the show moving along briskly. Slow song transitions or lengthy equipment changes can ruin the momentum of a good set. Make your presence known immediately to the audience. Grab their attention and never let it waver. Use your collaborative skills to gather the audience up in a mesmerizing web of music, sensibility, and personality.

Think about playing your best material right away. If you save it for last, you may not have an audience left to hear it, depending on your start time. If you are waiting for the crowd to get bigger, play it both times, first and last, but vary the delivery somewhat. Set lengths vary from 30–60 minutes in clubs or 30–120 minutes in concert halls and stadiums. Bands play covers to add bulk to their set lists until they have a repertoire of hits. Well-chosen covers can actually enhance your original material.

Bands need to set higher standards for themselves. If you make an effort to present a great show every time, you will become accustomed to the *routine* of a great show. When you slack off and only "get up" for big shows, you will have an incomplete foundation for

Nadine Sez

Grace Slick—essence of presence

Grace Slick is the most incredible live performer I have ever seen, bar none. She made it look simple. But working closely with her throughout the '80s, I knew the hard work and penultimate professionalism with which she approached her job.

Grace's natural stage presence was something that just couldn't be formulated or bought. She would do nothing but walk out onstage and own the room. Although Mickey Thomas had a much better voice and could sing rings around her, Grace controlled the crowd in a way Mickey could never achieve. I saw her stare down entire crowds of 20,000. She had that elusive, magical, mysterious "it." She was fascinating to watch, night after night.

Once I was taking Grace back to the dressing room after a series of TV interviews in the side rooms of the Meadowlands Coliseum in New Jersey. We inadvertently walked out the wrong door and into a crowd of fans leaving the concert. We were immediately rushed by about 100 fans who were getting hysterical upon seeing Grace. I began to panic but her sense of "presence" not only calmed me down, it taught me a valuable lesson. Presence is about self-control.

Cool and composed, Grace stopped and waited for the fans to come to her, pulling her autograph pen from her purse. Taking her cue, I informed the crowd that Grace would sign as many autographs as possible while we were leaving. Slowly and imperceptibly, I continued to walk her backwards toward the exit while she signed. I reassured the wild-eyed fans that they would get their autographs if they were patient and waited their turn. When we reached the exit door, I was able to open it and catch the eye of a security guard, who came out to help with the surging, impatient crowd. Then I caught the eye of the road manager, who came and brusquely whisked Grace away (his greatest asset) while I murmured apologies to the crowd and escaped backstage.

This was not long after John Lennon was slain, which is why I got so edgy in the rush of the crowd. All the crazies seemed to be coming out of the woodwork—we had already had a psychotic case try to burn down the venerable Starship Mansion where we worked. But Grace's presence (of mind), sense of self (self-preservation and self-control), and coolness saved the day.

the demands of live performance. You will find yourself unable to handle stage emergencies, unable to deal with recalcitrant crowds, and your presentation will remain uneven and inconsistent (the kiss of death). When a band has a good foundation and is not worrying about *how* they are playing onstage, *how* they look onstage, and *how* they sound onstage, then it frees them up to have significantly better shows.

Industry Showcases

If you are playing to an industry crowd, an adequate set length is 25–35 minutes. Play your best material and leave them wanting more. Don't make the mistake of playing too long and losing their interest. Less is generally more in those situations. Just because they are in the industry doesn't mean they have any longer attention spans than anyone else. In fact, it usually means their attention spans are shorter and much more jaded. Most industry reps simply want to see how you perform, your sense of style, how the audience reacts, and if you show potential. They are not looking to sign you on the spot.

If you are a band that generally needs a warm-up set, or your second show is generally your strongest set, then make arrangements to provide yourself with those opportunities so you make your best efforts when they count. I often tell bands to play *any* club the night before a big showcase, to get the butterflies out of their stomach and to make all their pacing errors and equipment mistakes when the industry won't see them.

An industry showcase is a terrible time to test out a new guitar or bass or a new song, although you will likely be using some gear that's already in the back line. Unfortunately, back lines are important in multiband showcases and we've all learned to live with them. Regardless of your situation, just do your best and use every opportunity as a learning experience. As mentioned, with very few exceptions (Counting Crows were one), bands generally don't get signed from showcases. In today's business climate, showcases generally serve as an introduction to a band and a chance to start or continue a dialogue with a label.

Critique of a Real Show

I was once a mentor of a band and had put them in a very good show-case slot on one of my Nadine's Wild Weekends. Unfortunately, they had equipment failure during their set and panicked, pretty much melting down the remainder of their set. Although there were high-level industry reps there specifically to see them, the response was tepid. No one was as impressed as I thought they could have been if they had seen a good show and recognized this band's potential. Several months later, I surprised the band at a gig to see how they were progressing. I wrote them the following e-mail the next morning with my thoughts about the show.

Hi Babydoll,

Great to see you last night. Here are my thoughts on the show...

Bad:

1. Very little has changed in the presentation since I saw you, and your entire presentation seemed very uninspiring.

2. The pacing of the set was poor . . . your first song is too slow to open a show . . . remember, you want to captivate them immediately. I think "song # 5" would be a better opener.

3. If you have to do vocal exercises to warm up first before you go on stage, so be it . . . do them, so you can do that better song first.

4. Your mid-set was excellent but then you ended flatly, with no ending punch and the show drizzled to a close.

5. You had little audience rapport. You were in the zone last night, but it wasn't with the audience.

6. Why is your guitar player (who has superstar potential) still buried in the back? Why don't you think of switching him and "the bass player" and also think of putting "the bass player" in sunglasses (glasses, dye job) to book-end "the keyboardist." The lead guitar is the other focal point to the lead singer. He should be next to you up

front. When "the bass player" takes his solo vocal, he can step up to the center mic.

7. Liked two out of the three new songs including the end one, but they all need work and I didn't really hear anything better than what you've recorded already. Keep writing, writing, writing—you can't write too much. The hit song that will put you over the top could be lurking in the new songs or right around the corner, or in something already recorded that gets re-recorded based on a new songwriting experiment.

8. By the way, you stank of B.O. Thank God I didn't have anyone with me . . . what is that about, buddy?

Good:

1. You, yourself, have something special and undefinable that can't be manufactured.

2. The band has an identifiable band sound, which is the envy of every band looking for its own voice.

3. You are all great players and you have crystal clear sound and tone.

4. Consistently good, good songs (but no "hit" songs).

You treated the show last night like a show in a dive bar. Although it *was* a show in a dive bar, you need to treat every show like A BIG DEAL . . . you never know who's going to be in the audience. I was there—what if I had brought [producer] Jerry Harrison or [producer] Rupert Hines with me?

One reason you had such problems with "your big showcase" during the Wild Weekend is that you aren't disciplining yourselves enough. If you treat every show consistently and make an effort to present a great show every time, you will become accustomed to the habit of a great show. You need to lay a better foundation for yourselves so your presentation is second nature, not something that distracts you. This will let your true talents shine.

Your songs mandate improvement from you. They are a cut above regular songs, but you look like just another regular band. If you think you are special, reflect that in your style, presentation, delivery, rapport. Who are you as a band? Last night's show did not reflect any personality except great ability to play. In this sound bite, visual music world of ours, where everyone has 30-second attention spans, that is not enough. Lots of people can play. *So what.* You want to give your audience MORE.

You don't want to blow the opportunity of your upcoming road trip by only having okay shows. You must have killer shows, where you grab them from the first note and leave them wanting more. Burn your show into their brains, so they remember you. Every show should be building your fan base.

And final bottom line is the songs...keep writing, writing, writing.... This is what artist development is about—hard work, making changes, and always challenging yourself to do better.

Glad I saw the show so I could critique it honestly.

Best,

Nadine

The band was a little taken aback by my *honesty* but took it in stride, since they knew I wouldn't have taken the time if I didn't care. I'm happy to say that one year after this, the same band had completed three regional multistate tours, successfully establishing themselves in other markets. They started making money on a regular basis and began flying to New York City for private showcases and private parties. Most importantly, they started making career decisions based on what was working for them. *This* is the meat of artist development. They still haven't written those hit singles but they are a steadily working, happy, and resourceful band.

One Band's Experience Buying Out a Club

One band I knew bought out a club so they could showcase for the manager of a huge supergroup. They called to invite me to the show and mentioned this manager was coming to see the band. I happened to be good friends with this supermanager.

I casually asked them when the show was and they said Sunday night of Memorial Day weekend. I knew that the manager was a family man who rarely went out on weekends. I also knew that he went out of town to his summer home every Memorial Day weekend. I asked if they were sure he was coming, after going to all the expense of renting the club and promoting the show. They were positive, since they had spoken to his office.

I called to tell him about the situation and he was appalled that someone in his office had committed him to seeing a band he didn't even know. Class act that he is, though, he went to fulfill the obligation. However, he did not think they were very good and probably resented being there.

The band was very disappointed after this experience. Although he did go see them, he passed on managing them. They were disappointed because, in their minds, their success or failure rode on this particular show and this particular manager agreeing to manage them. They had no plan beyond this show to fall back on, and the band project actually collapsed under the weight of their disappointment.

So focused were they on impressing the manager, that they lost sight of what they had really accomplished. The best thing that happened to this band, unbeknownst to them, was that they showed other clubs they could put a show together and draw several hundred people on a Sunday night of a three-day weekend (no small feat). That was a very good accomplishment right there, if they only could have recognized it.

Chapter 4 Keywords

1. **Promote**, **publicize**, and **produce** your own shows.
2. Think **outside the box** with alternative venues.
3. Make every show a **good** show.

Once you have begun to establish an identifiable sound and personality for your band through live performances, it's time to begin crafting your public persona through your Web site and publicity efforts. Chapter 5 concentrates on the importance of Web sites and smart publicity efforts.

REAL-WORLD SUCCESS STORY:

TV Rocker/Heartthrob Chris Isaak

When Chris Isaak was making his first record for Warner Brothers, *Chris Isaak and Silvertone,* I was working for Jefferson Starship and very casually dating one of Chris's managers, Mark Plummer. At that time, Starship was reinventing itself as a pop band. Los Angeles hair bands were just starting to come into vogue and new wave had given way to English dance music, which was storming the charts. To say that a retro-rockin' crooner from the Central Valley of California was not in fashion is an understatement.

In an effort to create a buzz around this modern but hard-to-define rock band, the managers put Chris in a very small club on Haight Street (which was a totally dead scene at that time). Mark, being English, had always fancied himself another Brian Epstein, and he had visions of Chris duplicating the Beatles' success at the Cavern Club. The Haight's Nightbreak held about 100 people total, with a stage the size of a postage stamp. Chris and his band established a "residency" on Thursday nights.

The first Thursday night, I was entertaining some friends in my apartment close to the club in the Upper Haight when I got a frantic call from the managers saying absolutely *no one* was at the club. I packed up my entire ten-person dinner party and moved them down the hill to the club. We were the only people in the room.

Chris was far from perfect that night. The set was shaky and herky-jerky, and the band was ragged. Rowland Salley, the bass player (who I had helped scout and convince to join the band), was brand new, and Chris was nervous. But Chris had such a distinctive style, such haunting songs, and such a droll sense of humor—I knew he was special. Kenney Dale Johnson, Rowland, and Jimmy Wilsey were all great players individually and showed they could get *in the groove, baby.* Rough as it was, it was *real rock 'n' roll* and my group had a blast.

Despite this inauspicious beginning, Chris and Silvertone kept at it every Thursday night. With Mark constantly browbeating everyone he ever met, people started to slowly trickle into the club to see Chris. Then Mark got girls to start coming. Whenever you can get girls to start showing up, the guys are not far behind. Lo and behold, Mark was starting a little scene. Soon, in cosmic fashion, it became "the" scene, just like Mark had hoped—packed with the sweaty bodies of rabid girl fans and "cooler-than-Steve McQueen" boys.

I had a little table in the front window that they always reserved for me, since it got so crowded. There was always a line, but I'd stroll right into the madness and chaos. As the months went by, I started seeing different industry personnel walk into the room. First Chris's local label rep, Warren Christianson, showed up, and then his regional reps and his national execs from Los Angeles to New York City. Shortly thereafter, his soon-to-be booking agents Dan Weiner and Fred Bollander started showing up.

This smart strategy allowed for things to happen in a cohesive, natural way. This was a very small club, so it always looked packed and that alone was fantastic. When you couldn't get in, you wanted in more than ever. It also gave Chris and his crackerjack band the perfect opportunity to refine and develop the show, since to that date Chris had not performed live very often. Although he was known to be a meticulous recorder (often note by note), the live situation was very new. Those Thursday nights playing in relative anonymity really helped him focus that unique Chris Isaak sound.

As the success and attention of that small sold-out club in the Haight swept over him, Chris was able to move on to a similar club in Los Angeles, the Anti Club, where he repeated the scenario. Every step of the way, he and his band mates had the opportunity to experience it, get used to it, and handle it. (The templates don't change!) Later they went to the infamous Danceteria in New York City and repeated the scenario again.

Chris had a lot of determination and heart. This was a very creative way to approach and lay a foundation for his career. It took a lot of courage to continue playing to nobody Thursday after Thursday after Thursday, until he started to create a draw.

I believe Chris using the Nightbreak experience to set the foundation of his career is one reason his band is still together (and on TV with him in Showtime's *The Chris Isaak Show*) after all these years. Although I never see Chris and Silvertone anymore, I'm crazy about their TV series and the story lines occasionally refer to those infamous Nightbreak shows. I was there! Good stuff.

REAL-WORLD SUCCESS STORY:

L3 (Live, Loud, and Local)

A San Francisco Bay Area band called the Matches has created one of the best independent, underage music scenes I've ever seen. Comprised of boys who attended the same high school in the East Bay, the band is brash, talented, and has unbounded youthful energy. Combining elements of pop, punk, and skateboarding, they present a slammin', crowd-pleasing show with hook-laden songs and dynamite stage presence. They are all developing into bona fide "players" led by the multitalented lead singer, Shawn Harris.

Like many other underage bands, the Matches were constantly frustrated by the lack of all-age venues. Even when they were booked into a 21-and-over nightclub, their fans could not attend the show. Instead of staying frustrated, the band started a monthly series called L3 (Live, Loud, and Local). They found a small Web casting auditorium called imusicast that was looking for exposure, was centrally located to where each band member lived, and had the technology to Web cast and video all their shows. The Matches recruited their parents to collect money at the door, sell sodas, and run lights. They invited other young, up-and-coming bands in the area including buzz bands Locale A.M., Solemite, and the K.G.B. (on the Dreamworks label) to play these shows with them. They did extensive street team and Internet marketing to their neighborhood fan base (all under 21, many under 18). They priced the shows very cheaply and started very early (6:00 P.M. start, over by 10:00 P.M.). Wow.

The next thing you knew, the Matches were drawing 300 to 400 kids to every show—making money, selling merchandise, and ratcheting up their word of mouth. They developed a community of kids where before there was a total void of activity. They watched their videotapes, critiqued themselves, and experimented. Now they are touring constantly, taking their concept of music and community on the road. They are content to sell their own records while working on new recordings and refining their sound. They will obtain a record deal, but no hurry. They're *young*. This is the true meat-and-potatoes of artist development. Good, good, stuff—and a very creative approach to an age-old problem (excuse the pun).

Create a Web Site, Make a Press Kit, Hire a Publicist

Introduction: Web Sites Are the No. 1 Resource Today

A band's Web site gives industry professionals and fans alike that all-important first look, first impression, first vibe. A&R reps, booking agents, nightclub managers, columnists, music reviewers, band managers, and fans often go to a music Web site before deciding to return a call, write a press blurb, or see a show. Web sites are the press kits of the twenty-first century. Easy to access and navigate, they are an immediate resource of unlimited information for bands, the press, audiences, and record buyers.

Too often I see sites that are outdated, don't tell an attention-getting story about the band, or bury pertinent information that the industry needs at the end of a long and basically boring bio. Remember, *you* tell us *why* we should listen to your music. We cannot guess what makes you special.

Press kits are synchronous to an artist's Web site in style and design. Press kits serve as abbreviated hard copies of succinct information derived from the Web site. They also often contain tactile and tangible items related to the promotion of the artist. Most press kits contain an actual CD and some piece of brand merchandising (button, poster, banner) to help us remember the band.

It's imperative that you define who you are to the industry. Because of the sheer amount of product sent out, no one has the time, initially, to discern what makes you special or to determine the best song on the record. No one has the time, on the first pass, to listen to the whole record, read your entire bio, and look at all your press clips. But everyone is looking for that *hint* of potential in each pile of CDs that makes them take a closer look, listen more intently, research the band more completely. Make your music presentation stand out from the stack.

This chapter will help you develop two powerful tools that help set you apart from the crowd: your Web site and your press kit. You will learn how to stop being just another band with your hand out looking for a deal—by establishing a Web site that reflects the band accurately and highlights your accomplishments, and developing a tag line, logo, and style. You will learn better ways to describe your music, what makes a good story, what goes into a press kit, and the basics of media opportunities. By the end of this chapter, you'll be able to talk about your project more confidently, knowing you have reliable source materials at your fingertips, both on the Web and in hard copy.

Make Your Web Site Home Page the Hook

Set the tone of your music with your home page. Bring out the band's personality online. Your Web site is an extension of your CD cover, your recording style, and your live show. It should be an accurate and compelling reflection of all three. A good home page makes the Internet user stop what they are doing and open other pages on your site for more detailed information. Make the home page dynamic, expressive, creative, and accessible, featuring the stamp of your personality.

Hook the Web surfer with smashing news. Link these "headlines" to your other pages, which will contain more substantial information. The bells and whistles of Flash pages are entertaining but not nearly as valuable as listing relevant career facts. Here are 16 possible

Nadine Sez

Madonna

Madonna is the most incredible person I've ever watched handle the press. From persona to persona, she defines her story on her terms, attracts your attention, and pulls the interviewer, reader, viewer, and fan into her music, style, and story. A marketing genius, she consistently redefines her image for each new release, thereby ensuring her fans will not tire of her message. Most importantly, she backs it all up with music that does nothing but sell, sell, sell. You can't just have the marketing image with no music substance. What a one-two punch. What a master of design.

I'll never forget the very first MTV Music Awards, when I was standing on the side of the stage of Radio City Music Hall with an all-access pass. Mickey Thomas and Grace Slick were award presenters and I was working backstage with them. While millions watched on television, I stood there open-mouthed watching Madonna roll around the floor in that wedding dress. Absolutely brilliant. Totally audacious. She wasn't so beautiful then, and her talent wasn't as well defined as it is now, but her personality was so forceful you couldn't *not* watch her. Her unabashed self-confidence was captivating.

It was Cyndi Lauper's bad luck to be performing the same night. Although she had a much better voice, her "Girls Just Want to Have Fun" routine paled in comparison to Madonna's over-the-top, sexy performance. I think that's when MTV really came into it's own as the compelling new music medium.

items to highlight on a home page that speak to both the industry and consumers:

1. Recorded samples of your music
2. CD sales figures
3. Opening slot for major headliner
4. Touring activities
5. Regular gig schedule with upcoming dates
6. Working with a name producer
7. Recording your music in a special technological way
8. Recording your music in a certain musical style
9. Recording your music with unique instrumentation
10. Radio airplay in any market
11. Good press reviews
12. Fan comments and testimonials
13. Guest books for Web site visitors
14. Online promotions such as CD or ticket giveaways
15. Number of Web site downloads
16. Number of Web site hits

Consider highlighting these items with bullet points. Flag that great opening slot for Matchbox Twenty. Emphasize a special producer who worked on a few tracks. Inform your reader that you have radio airplay. Post up-to-date information on timely news: CD sales, gig info, quantity of downloads to date, and online promotions. Don't forget to highlight your interactive hooks, whether they are your placement on other sites, sign-ups and guest books, or fan reviews. Demonstrate your resourcefulness by running special promotions or setting up your own shows and publicizing them on the site.

Develop a Tag Line, Logo, and Style

Take the initiative in describing your music in a short, catchy way that is easy for people to remember and identify with you. Develop a tag line ("The New Rock Alternative," "Rock's Savior," "Punk Darlings") that defines your music, style, attitude, and effort. This is a phrase or sentence that accurately describes your sound but is also enticing enough to grab people's attention.

A band's logo will be repeated over and over on decals, stickers, album art, T-shirts, flyers, posters, and Web sites in an effort to position the band in people's consciousness. Think of designing your logo with an eye toward these multiple applications. Design these catchy collaterals in synch with your tag line.

Logos are used for at least the life of a record (which is a minimum of one year to three years). The standard amount of time per logo is 24–36 months. Remember, logos are your visual sound bites. Everyone needs a visual reference in today's modern world. We all live in an MTV-influenced society of short sound bites, quick cuts, and quick burn factors. Designing a good logo and style provides the reassuring consistency necessary in today's overamped marketing arenas that follow fad to fad.

Define Your "Story"

Develop an interesting story about your band/project that will set you apart from the crowd. The information that you have recorded a CD or are performing live does not warrant much interest in today's overcrowded marketplace. Think about what distinguishes you from being just another needy band looking for a deal, an audience, or a review.

An interesting story consists of elements of fact and fiction that are attention grabbing. It must be compelling enough to make someone want to know more about the band. Tell people what makes you special. Initially you might focus on these things:

- Unusual backgrounds of the band members
- Intriguing recording instruments
- Unique style of recording
- Special studio setting
- Special producer or engineer
- Guest musicians
- Songwriting collaborations with established professionals
- Internet and fanzine reviews

Later you will want to expand with:

- Well-attended live shows
- Special upcoming show
- Unique onstage delivery
- Regional tour
- Regional college airplay
- CD sales
- Internet traffic
- Press quotes and reviews

Developing your own story means giving the press something to write about. Remember to answer the basic "who, what, when, where, why, and how" questions.

Ask yourself what noteworthy events have happened to the band recently. Any dynamic opening slots for major stars? Any good quotes from radio or other press? Clearly point out what makes you so special (first record, name producer, live recording, guest musicians). Give the basics: Who are you and what is your background and history? What are you doing and where do you live and record? Why did you make this record, start a band, hire that producer, write that song, play that show, team up with that band? How is this band/performance/record different from any other record? What sets you apart from the crowd? Explain the significance of choosing a certain producer or why your shows are unique.

If you don't have an interesting story, create one. Like the time you recorded music that stopped traffic; played the local high school in parochial school uniforms; crashed an in-store for Incubus and played three songs; threw your demo tape over the brick wall of Bruce Springsteen's estate; impersonated the Foo Fighters on a call-in radio show. Make your story an adventure, a fable, a superhero's tale. Ultimately you want someone to listen to your music. You are confident that once they listen to your music, they will like it. But first, you must cut through the melee of modern life and get their attention.

Describe Your Music

Can you describe your music *simply* and *accurately*? It's not only *who* you sound like, it's also *what* you sound like and in *which genre* of music. *Who* you sound like is a good start for defining your genre. Pick better-known bands realistically, though, in terms of actual style (it's almost impossible to sound like Moby *and* Crosby, Stills & Nash). Most bands are too broad in their selections. Pick just two artists that influence your sound and leave it at that.

What your band sounds like should be as factual as possible. Describe your music *simply* (so it's easy to understand and absorb) and *accurately* (so reviewers, DJs, club bookers, or producers don't feel misled when they listen to it). Many bands describe their music in extremely vague terms, using too many words. Make a simple, declarative statement. A paragraph description is generally too long. Two succinct sentences usually works well.

Examples of music descriptions that help convey a mood or style are melodic songs; bombastic sound; crunching chords; crushing drums; ethereal vocals; complex song structures; mature songwriting; fresh, clean, crisp vocals; cohesive playing; guitar-heavy; snaky bass lines; percussive unit; groove-oriented songs; stunning blend of voices; impressive songwriting ability.

Picking a genre is for those who are more sophisticated and want to use music industry lingo. The industry describes music only in terms of radio genres, so be prepared to learn about Triple A (Adult Album Alternative), alternative, active rock, Hot AC (Adult Contemporary) dance, and Top 40. Current terminology defining music that may be brilliant but deemed unsuitable for commercial radio airplay is delineated as indie, underground, jam band, or college radio–oriented.

20 Possible Web Page Categories

Music Web site categories might include any of the following: home page, bio, news, history, meet the band, albums, videos, photos, tour dates and gigs, newsletters, press pages, media kits, merchandise, buy CD, song clips, message boards, guest books, links, street teams, fan clubs, and contests. *Be sure to link all pages to and from the home page.*

1. **Bio** of the band can remain static as long as the personnel don't change. Limit the time frame to the last five years. Do not talk about grade school or high school, unless you were performing professionally at that time, won music awards, or were singled out for special attention. Focus on what makes you and your music unique, special, and apart from the rest.

2. **News** should be any activity of note from the last three months or coming up in the next three months, giving you a moving six-month window. (The only exception to this rule might be posting a gig list of the last 6–12 months *if* you were active enough—everyone likes to see a working band.) Press releases, new photos, CD sales figures, and sold-out shows can all go on this page.

3. **History** can archive older information, past press clips, past gig lists, and such, making them accessible but not the focus. Anything older than three years should be archived.

4. **Meet the band** photos can present the individual members. This is also a good place to have individual bio facts and personalized info on the members.

5. **Albums** can talk about all the past albums, but make sure you focus on your current album and have a "Buy CD" button on that page or linking to the buy page.

6. **Videos** from unsigned bands often show a lot of creativity and generally are a gas to watch. Whether they fall into the category of home movies or future MTV classics, they rock.

7. **Photos** must include one black-and-white horizontal shot in a format that newspapers and magazines can download with ease. A "print quality" .tiff or .jpeg is generally good for this. Live shots are good for keeping your site dynamic and fresh. Showing your fans in your live shots keeps them coming back to your site and bringing their friends.

8. **Tour dates and gigs** are important for two immediate reasons: Your fans know where you are playing so they can support your shows, and the industry sees that you are popular enough to be playing on a regular basis. This site category also tells the industry what quality of clubs you have been playing and how much of your time is spent performing.

9. **Newsletters** are a good way of keeping in touch with your e-mail lists of fans and industry contacts. They are most effective on a monthly basis.

10. **Press pages** can hold scanned feature articles on the band or links to published articles or reviews. Pull the best quotes and post those on the home page for more attention-getting power.

11. **Media kits** should include printable downloads of your one-page band bio, a page of media quotes, and a black-and-white band photo shot horizontally.

12. **Buy CD** is possibly the most important aspect of your site. It's best to have the "Buy CD" button on every page of your site.

13. **Merchandise** can be an added source of income. Merch can also help build your branding awareness to the general public while offering your fans items that they can't find anywhere else!

14. **Song clips** are imperative so site visitors can hear your music immediately. If your music is compelling enough, it will force the listener to navigate through more of the site, go to a show, or buy the record online. Whether these clips are 30 seconds long or full downloads is up to you, but they should be long enough to garner a full effect.

15. **Message boards** are a good interactive way to foster artist-fan conversations, making your fans feel involved. Many artists—including Mariah Carey, Courtney Love, and Fred Durst (Limp Bizkit)—actually chat with their fans on a regular basis.

16. **Guest books** are another way to create Internet activity with fans and can serve to spotlight your growing popularity.

17. **Links** to other sites—whether Amazon.com, another band's site, or a Webzine you are crazy about—are de rigueur if you want the casual, surfing fan to find you.

18. **Street teams** serve to get fans involved by bringing them onto your "team" to help promote your activities to their friends in their neighborhoods.

19. **Fan clubs** are generally reserved for major label bands with label staff who maintain the club's administration.

20. **Contests** are a wide-open way to flex your creativity on the business end. They can offer tickets to shows, a ride to a gig

with the band, the chance to meet the lead singer's Mom, or any other silly yet eye-catching promotion.

The newer the band, the fewer the pages. Don't be intimidated by trying to combine pages and put the stamp of your personality on each one. There are no set rules on the Web as far as content and design go, but I think you must start with at least these four key pages:

Home page: Position your logo prominently, put up your CD artwork, and have a sign-up box for your e-mail list.

Bio page: Provide one good black-and-white band photo and a bio that prints out to one page, using double-spaced typing.

News page: List your past and upcoming gigs, and consider getting quotes from other bands or fans in lieu of press quotes (unless you have some).

Buy CD page: Try to have a commercial system in place so you can take credit cards and put your MP3 songs on this page.

Make Your Site Interactive and Trackable

I believe creating Internet activity with your fans makes them feel a part of your special happening scene and music. It's one aspect of the widespread personal communication the Internet affords all of us. Commit your Internet audience by getting them involved. Asking fans to request additional info, attend a show, or become part of the music "family" incorporates them into your success. Enticing viewers to interact with you on some level gives them a personal attachment to the project. Not only is it a great informational tool but a way to "sell through" down the line when you have new product or merch. Being able to rely on your e-mail list to turn out bodies for an important show is invaluable. Remember to leave Internet viewers *wanting* something more from you, whether it's a fans-only, specially burned CD or tickets to an out-of-town show.

Internet activity is also a good way to accentuate the response your music is getting online. Knowing how many hits your Web site garners each day, week, and month is valuable ammunition for your promotional arsenal. Selling CDs online through a commercial system is indisputable evidence of your ability to sell your music.

Top Four Site Sins

1. Failing to put your "Buy CD" click-through and e-mail list sign-up box on *every* page! Viewers do not always enter your site via the home page and surf in orderly fashion. You will dramatically increase your CD sales and list of e-mail addresses with this simple activity.

2. Highly visible outdated material and information. People are interested in what you are doing *now*. Consider archiving these older items for those who may want more information. Rule of thumb is to archive anything over three years old, possibly even two. (This means we don't care what happened in the year 2000, no matter how good it was—if it was *that* good, you'd be signed by now.)

Nadine Sez

Get out of the band ghetto

Get out of the band ghetto by explaining what sets you apart from the crowd. Stop being just another band looking for a deal—highlight your accomplishments. Well-attended live shows, a regional tour, college airplay, CD sales, Internet sales, press quotes, and album reviews are all activities that show you are interesting, unusual, and serious about your career.

Many bands are unable to distill who they are and how they sound into an easy-to-understand statement. When asked to name their best song, they can't even do that. Point out the best things about your band and create a tag line that will resonate in people's brains. Make your tag easy to remember so people identify you with your shows, your record, your site, your vibe.

Consider this scenario: A music writer receives two CDs of music by two different bands. The music is the same quality on both—very decent. CD-A has a clever press kit that promotes a thoughtful, fun Web site packed with information, while CD-B's kit has an incomplete bio and the band's site hasn't been updated in six months. Both bands want a mention for an upcoming show. The reviewer has space for only one. Which CD will he pick? (CD-A)

3. Old band photos that don't show the current, accurate lineup. (Nothing is worse than telling an agent over the phone what a fox your new lead singer is, while the agent stares at an old band photo sans the foxy singer.)

4. Boring, long-winded bios that say nothing germane to your cause. The bio can remain static as long as band personnel don't change, but please—it is not necessary to start at age five with your interest in music. (We all played with Mr. Microphone, sister!)

Use the Power of the World Wide Web

Remember: Singers, musicians, and bands are the *content providers.* Take advantage of the wealth of *content-hungry* sites out there. Post your music and info on your music on as many sites as possible. Don't stop at the standard fare—look for wildly creative, diverse, intriguing music and band sites. Use the Internet as your own personal promotional tool. Research the plethora of Webzines, sites, and newsletters that cater to your fan base, age group, and genre. The Web is a powerful tool. Educate yourself on its possibilities.

Smash Mouth reaches out to its fans through its fun and informative Web site, just as singer Steve Harwell is connecting with the audience here in one of the band's dynamic live shows.

Create Your Press Kit

A good press kit takes the essence of your story from the Web site to describe why your music or your project is important. It flags upcoming activities in press release form and establishes why they are of interest to the press and their audiences. It supplies concise bio information applicable to both press and fans. It highlights significant band members and explains why they are noteworthy. It suggests the three best tracks on your record for listening purposes and why they are the three best tracks.

By defining who you are accurately, you are fulfilling your partnership with the press. They need to know this information, and it's your job to give it to them clearly and succinctly. They are looking for content of interest, and you are the provider of that content.

A press kit should be more specific than a Web site. Since every person who will receive your kit is inundated by paper and extraneous materials, keep to the particulars. Constantly refer them to your Web site, which should contain greater depth of information. In today's world, press kits are the front door key, but Web sites are the whole house.

A good press kit contains the following:
- Your most recent CD
- A "cover letter" written in press release form outlining current activities
- A one-page bio
- Two good black-and-white photos
- Specific quotes pulled from press reviews (can be on the back side of the bio)
- Suggestions of tracks to listen to that are well marked on the CD

Once again, keep your bio current. Unless you have achieved a modicum of success, no one cares what you did five years ago. Be careful not to date yourself with old quotes that are *irrelevant* to your current project. Consider making your music disc a CD-ROM so you can include your bio, photos, reviews, even video, all on one disc that's convenient to research and easy to store.

Highlight press reviews with "pull quotes"—the best quotes pulled directly from the text of a review or other legitimate source. Often bands include complete articles, reviews, or interviews, but no one has the time to read these through at first glance. It is best to post the articles in their entirety on your Web site and inform the reader of their availability there. List quotes by newspaper, magazine, or radio station, and include the publication or airplay date. These pull quotes will convey the legitimacy of the press, while being snappy enough to get readers' attention.

Remember to KISS (Keep It Simple, Stupid). In this fast-paced world of ours, you need to be as simple, clear, and concise as possible to be considered for anything. No one has the time or inclination to paw through pounds of material looking for the right description, right photo, or right quote. No one has the time to wade through your press packet to figure out who you are. No one has the time to listen to 12 songs to guess your sound. Simple, focused, direct facts are best.

Give out the information you've determined is the right information. This right information should consist of a tag line, a story, an image, a sound—all rendered consistently. Keep refreshing people's memories about who and what you are. Include the Web site URL on every piece of paper.

Another Word on Photos

The best press photos show the band members' faces. Everyone (newspapers, magazines, booking agents, A&R reps, mangers, and clubs) likes to see what a band looks like and whether the players are young, old, cute, punky, hardcore, pretty, hot, funky, pierced, tattooed, alternative, long haired, short haired, bearded, bald, girls, boys…. So, as mentioned, you need two straight-ahead, black-and-white shots (one horizontal, one vertical) that *actually show the band.* Keep those arty, atmospheric, symbolic shots for the album cover, liner notes, or Web site.

Always put the star of the band front and center. Always put the best-looking members up front. If your star is unattractive, put that person up front with good-looking people on either side. Play up the difference by making it arresting. This is one area where I do not believe in democracy. I can't tell you the countless photos I've seen with the star in the back, behind a lackluster lineup. No matter what bond you have with your fellow players, no matter what emotional support you share, and no matter how indebted you are to them, a photo is not the time for equality. I'm against it. This is business.

Make sure you put your phone number on the back of the photo. It's also very helpful to put the band's name and, if there is room, the band members' names right on the photo itself, so the media has the correct spellings at hand. While most press still prefer black-and-white glossy prints, many media outlets are now adept at digital downloading. Be sure, though, that your online photo is in the right format (.tiff or .jpeg), and that you can supply a 300 dpi version.

Research the Media

Do your research. In this information age, there is more accessibility to lists of reviewers, newspaper staffs, and magazine staffs than ever before. Do your homework and research these names in advance. Target the right reviewers and writers. Determine in advance who has similar tastes to yours and reviews similar projects. Assess who may be sympathetic to the project prior to your mailing.

Send your press kit to appropriate, genre-specific writers. Do not send it to writers across the board. When you send it to inappropriate writers, generally it gets thrown away. Don't send your punk record to the country reviewer. You deserve to treat your product better. No one has so many self-produced CDs that they can afford to have them discarded due to poor advance research.

Reflect on what magazine, fanzines, and music newspapers you read yourself. Assess your story realistically in light of their editorial direction. Consider contacting them if you have a story appropriate for their readership.

Call or e-mail them with regular updates on your musical activities. Your consistency and professionalism will sway them, if space opens up.

Consider initiating publicity opportunities for yourself. Quit playing the same boring shows. Bring in special guests, or have your famous producer sit in for a set. Get the correct legal permits and set up your band in the mall or in the parking lot of a huge concert, or stage a kamikaze play-in at City Hall (be creative, but make sure it's legal!). Contact the press in advance and contact them again with the follow-up story.

When to Hire a Publicist

Bands get into a conundrum over when to hire a publicist and how much to pay him or her. Most bands can handle their own publicity in the beginning. Writing your own press release and bio is an excellent exercise in determining the best qualities of your music and analyzing what makes you unique. However, there are certain situations where a publicist may be beneficial: specific tasks, short-term projects, a national release, and a performing tour.

Specific tasks

Often you can hire a publicist for a specific task, such as writing your bio or a press release, placing a particular photo or item in a newspaper, or coordinating a photo shoot. The publicist completes only that precise activity and is not concerned with any other aspect of the overall project. If you're an unsigned band, these are good options that can help launch you in the right direction for a reasonable fee. Reading a professionally written bio can help you decide what information should be included in your press release, and vice versa. Plus, publicists often have photographer friends and are good conduits for band photos. Expect to pay by the task, ranging from $150–$500.

Short-term projects

Examples of short-term (about three months) projects for a publicist are mailing your CD to a specific press review list and following up, soliciting Web-only reviews and items, or providing radio airplay information to the trade magazines. These activities require more finesse and generally involve more professional contacts than are accessible to the general public. You are paying a publicist for the accuracy of their mailing lists, the caliber of their contacts, and the professional reputation he or she has garnered. Expect to pay by the project, ranging from $500 (for a small, region-specific mailing of 20 CDs or less) to $5,000.

A national release

It's ridiculous to release a record with national distribution without publicizing it. But unless you have a stupendous story, the simple fact that you are releasing a record may not be enough to get the newspaper or magazine space you desire. You need to build excitement around the record in advance of its release: fantastic music, rave advance reviews from industry insiders or other well-known

Invest in your band name

*M*any a band stuck in the frustrating mid-career doldrums will consider changing their name. Generally I think this is a bad idea, for several reasons.

One, a band builds value into a name through their hard work and efforts. There is branding association attached to a band's name for merchandise sales and marketing value. Since it takes so long for a band to seep into the public's consciousness, it is the continual repetition of the band's name in advertising, on CDs, on the Internet, and elsewhere that is the cohesive thread to recognition.

Two, building a fan base around a certain band creates that core constituency so valued by the industry. It's impossible to gauge accurately the value of fan loyalty. Changing the name in midstream is not only confusing, but may also denigrate this fan loyalty.

A great example of a how a band almost changed its name disastrously is the case of Jefferson Starship. As you know, this band was founded by Paul Kantner and Grace Slick of Jefferson Airplane. Paul had already recorded his first solo record, though, *Blows Against the Empire,* and took to calling the varied assortment of musicians who played on it (Jerry Garcia, David Crosby, Grace, and many others) Jefferson Starship.

Although he had built up a tremendous amount of currency and name recognition with Jefferson Airplane, Paul wanted a brand-new name for the band. But Bill Thompson, Paul's manager, saw that it was illogical to dismiss the branding and fan tradition associated with Jefferson Airplane and finally convinced Paul to use Jefferson Starship. In later years, after Paul left Jefferson Starship, that name was legally retired and the remaining members (including Grace) continued on as simply Starship.

artists, obtaining a major manager, or securing the services of a top booking agency. Publicists who run these campaigns try to secure TV appearances, mentions or reviews, national magazine reviews and features, trade publication stories, or radio convention appearances, and pitch syndicated writers. These publicists also work the media in the top cities: New York City, Los Angeles, San Francisco, Seattle, San Diego, Phoenix, Denver, Minneapolis, Boston, Chicago, Detroit, Atlanta, St. Louis, Miami, Philadelphia, New Orleans, Kansas City, Nashville, Houston, Dallas, and Cleveland. Expect the campaign to run three months initially and extend every three months if things are going well. Expect to pay by the month, anywhere from $1,000–$5,000 per month.

A performing tour

Any tour, regardless of length, is a positive time to hire a publicist. A tour publicist can advance your dates from town to town to make sure your show is spotlighted, your current album is reviewed with a link to the show, or the actual show is reviewed (in hopes of generating post-show record sales.) Having a publicist call a newspaper about your upcoming appearance is a sign of a well-organized, professional band. Some bands however, like those in the jam band scene, rarely use a publicist because they can sell out on their own in each market. If you can sell out in a market, don't waste your money using a publicist. For the rest of us, tour publicists are golden. They usually like to have an 8- to 12-week lead time before the tour starts plus one month after it ends. Expect to pay by the month, anywhere from $1,000–$5,000 per month.

In conclusion, try to work with publicists who are on your own level. It's silly to hire a national publicist when you don't have any national commercial airplay or national distribution. Always try to work out a reduced project fee with your publicist, as opposed to a monthly fee. Publicists often have record label clients paying them larger fees. Since they have to call these media outlets anyway, they can take on smaller, more personal projects for less money.

Because of the fickle nature of the media, there is never any guarantee of media placement, despite what you may be paying a publicist. Start with small, short-term projects that will give you the chance to see how well you work with a publicist. You are paying for his or her time to call and pitch your project to appropriate media outlets.

Before hiring a publicist, sit down to discuss what you hope to achieve. Be clear about your goals and your priorities. Look at the publicist's mailing list and other clients. Ask for client references and media contacts. Are the contacts appropriate for your media campaign? It's great if your publicist works with jam bands, but what if you are an alternative, indie rocker? Ask the publicist to time line a publicity plan. Retain the right to change your publicist if things aren't working to your specifications. Renewable, short-term media campaigns are best, so you can accurately gauge the success to date before committing more money.

Be careful not to lock yourself into costly, ineffective media campaigns. I knew one independent label that paid over $35,000 to a Los Angeles firm over a year's time and got *two mentions* (not even full sentences). Holy Cow, what a scam! I would have stopped after $5,000 and three months as reasonable assessment of a national campaign. If you are not seeing the results you clearly prioritized in advance, or you can't get the publicist on the phone, those are red flags to stop and reassess the campaign.

Chapter 5 Keywords

1. **Review your materials regularly** to keep them current. Outdated facts, photos, and information spoil a good effort. Photos with band members who left last year mar your presentation and subtly alter how the industry perceives you.
2. List a **working phone number** with a professional message center. The only thing worse than receiving a CD, demo, or press kit with no phone number is a disconnected phone number. Include your snail mail, e-mail, and Web site addresses.
3. **Pay attention to detail!** Misspellings, incorrect club addresses, erroneous start times, and bungled talent listings all make for a sloppy introduction to the industry.
4. **Handle your own publicity** for as long as possible. It will give you the best feel for what is working and what isn't.
5. There is never a guarantee of **media placement.** Be realistic about your campaigns and the money you are spending.

Nadine Sez

Band Web sites and the Internet

*I*t's impossible for me to pick just a few band Web sites to use as successful examples. I am constantly impressed and delighted by the broad range of styles and personalities I find on music Web sites, whether nationally known bands, or completely independent ventures. All the bands mentioned in this book have great but widely diverse sites.

The best sites I see, in any genre, are the sites that sell CDs and tickets to shows, have message boards, post updated information weekly (if not more often), and basically are "living" sites with interactive properties.

As an industry veteran, I look for facts and figures to support the music. But as a fan, I look for personality and the music itself. As a fan, I want to be part of something special. I like a site that makes me feel part of the inner circle. I also like being offered music, specials, merchandise, and tickets in advance of the general public. That's worth getting newsletters, updates, and all the other band-generated e-mail, and it helps retain my loyalty.

The explosion of Apple iTunes, along with paid Internet downloads being tracked as legitimate retail sales, has finally brought the industry and the Internet together for the first real foray into legitimate downloading. It may not be a marriage made in heaven, but it is a marriage of necessity for the twenty-first century.

By eliminating the manufacturing and distribution obstacles that have stymied many an artist, the Internet has truly made the music business a level playing field for all contenders. This is the true power of the Internet. Whether you harness it personally or market behind it, the Internet will continue to redefine popular entertainment for the remainder of our lives and beyond.

6

Record a Demo CD, Work with a Producer, Woo Radio Airplay

Introduction: What Is a *Hit* Song?

A *hit* song is any song in any genre that gets an *immediate* positive reaction. A hit song elicits a physical reaction from the listener, whether it be singing along to the radio, calling the radio station to find out who it was, turning on MTV to catch the video, going into a record store to buy the song, surfing online to find the artist's Web site, or going to see the artist play live. Hit songs come in all styles and all colors, but the one thing they all have in common is they all get an *immediate* response.

Spending money does not ensure a hit song. Recording in an expensive studio with a lot of overdubs and production effects cannot mask a weak, ineffective song. It's not *how much* money you spend on the recording. It's *how well* the song is written, played, or sung. I've heard demos that songwriters sang into little tape recorders in their living rooms and demos that cost as much as many fully realized commercial records. Poor songwriting is still poor songwriting, no matter how you cloak it.

Demos exist to show that the artist can sing, play, and write a song. Demos can be two songs or 14 songs, self-produced or professionally produced, recorded on 4-track or 64-track or live to DAT. But what demos can't be is boring, muffled, and poorly marked.

This chapter will explore what makes a good demo, the value of a producer and how to find one. After you record your music, you are confronted with how to get people to hear it. I'll tackle the fact and fiction world of radio promotion and give some strategies for alternatives to airplay. I'll tell you about the most amazing demos I've ever heard (by Counting Crows) and share my Starship stories.

ABCs of Recording a Demo CD

Focus on the song. Hit songs drive every aspect of the music industry. Record a demo in the best way that conveys the song. It's the *song* that should stand out, not the production. Don't let overproduction distract from a song. While the majority of labels expect a certain type of recording quality from artists today, music professionals can hear a good song in any format, from acoustic to electric, 4-track to 64-track system. But with the accessibility of inexpensive digital recording tools, a recording of professional quality is available to most everyone.

Singers and musicians looking for session or touring gigs do take a different approach to recording demos. Singers should make sure their vocals stand out effectively instead of getting buried in the mix. Singers should also nix the drum and guitar solos. If you are selling your voice, then that is what folks will want to hear. If you are a player looking for a gig, then the recording can be instrumentally expressive and stylistically varied. But most musicians use their band recordings and then audition in person.

Quit Reworking a Song to Death

Every band can write one really good song that gets people's attention and gets a reaction. The secret is to write *five great songs* after that. If you've recorded a song professionally two times the best way you know how, it's time to let it go and move on. Songs are not children. You're not going to have just two. In fact, you can

Nadine Sez

Radio rarity Luce

*L*uce is one independent band who used the Triple A (Adult Album Alternative) radio format successfully to advance their career. This is a textbook example of luck, timing, and having the right song at the right time. This Bay Area band was able to garner radio airplay before obtaining a label contract—a rarity in the radio world. It all came about when Tom Luce's brother passed on the Luce demo to Joe Schuld, a veteran radio promoter with Columbia Records. After Joe left Columbia, he began managing Luce and repackaged the demo into a full-length release. Working as an independent radio promoter for Luce, Joe asked the San Francisco Triple A radio station KFOG to listen to the album.

Liking what they heard, KFOG added "Good Day" and "Long Way Down" to their playlist. Through this airplay, Luce was able to expand their local audience and attract airplay on other top stations across the country. Thanks to Joe's business savvy, his experience, and his excellent contacts in radio, the band had 30 stations playing their music before they signed a recording contract with Nettwork Records.

After they signed with Nettwork, Luce toured the country playing concerts and festivals sponsored by these same stations. "Good Day" ultimately peaked at No. 35 on the radio charts and was the 37th most-played song on Triple A radio in 2002.

have hundreds. You can always go back to that one song later, after you've written more.

A major stumbling block for many, many bands is that the first good song they write is also their first song to get any legitimate reaction. So they keep re-recording it, hoping it will become a hit. But that time spent re-recording would be better off spent writing new (potentially *hit)* songs. If it's not a positive hit immediately with a professional, then rarely does another producer or studio make enough of a difference to warrant the additional cost and effort. Also keep in mind that if you do sign a major label deal, the label will most likely make you record the songs anew anyway—so why spend your own money?

Budget Considerations for the Quantity of Songs

Do your homework to ensure you have the appropriate cost information for your project and then budget accordingly. It would not make sense to spend tens of thousands of dollars on your first demo effort. Familiarize yourself with the recording process and make sure you have an oeuvre of proven songs before you commit to more costly recording activities. Studio recording is more akin to gambling than creativity...fun but expensive, and boy—how time flies! Although my studio friends won't be happy with me for saying this, be careful of these money pits.

Budgets can vary widely in this age of digital recording. Generally, first-time demos of a couple of songs are in the $500–$1,000 range. Working with a more established name or studio will run about $2,500 per song. An indie project shouldn't run over $25,000–$30,000 for a full album of songs.

Don't forget to budget for the hidden costs of tape or discs, rented equipment, sound enhancements, overtime, and additional personnel. Most recordings take *twice* as long as you allotted. Remember the 25 percent reserves rule in padding your budget.

Consider recording only your best material instead of a full album. Two good songs will be more productive than ten mediocre ones. Unless you are recording a full album to sell online and at shows, limit your recordings to two to five songs. (You can also sell a five-song EP online and at shows.) One thing to remember is that no matter how much a professional likes your songs, you will always be asked if you have *any more songs recorded.* Consider releasing your best songs in a calculated, deliberate manner that will pique and hold a pro's interest.

Many producers work on speculation ("spec"). This means they absorb all the costs of production in exchange for either a flat fee or a royalty payment when the record is sold to a record company. Often times they own production companies that cover the cost of recording in exchange for the exclusive rights to the finished product. In essence they act as subcontractors. They take the finished record and license it to major labels for marketing and distribution. Working on spec is a perfectly viable option for many struggling artists, *as long as the terms are fair to both parties.* I generally discourage artists from signing deals with production companies that include *both* management *and* publishing percentages. It's better to let managers handle the management, producers produce the songs, and publishers market and collect licensing fees.

Packaging a Demo CD

Make sure your name is clearly readable on your CD cover. Put your name in legible font, both horizontally along the top front and vertically along the spine. This will guarantee that whether I'm flipping through a pile of CDs on my desk or scanning CDs in a record store bin, your name is obvious and I can find your CD.

You *must* put your phone number on your CD cover, along with your e-mail, Web site, and snail mail address. Also imprint or handwrite this information directly on the disc. With multidisc players so popular today, it's easy for CDs to get separated from their cases.

The insert or back cover should list the songs in the song order. More often than not I have to counsel bands on listing their tracks, since the only song documentation is on the CD inside my player.

Additional information that is beneficial but not mandatory is song length, the band's photo, songwriting credits, song lyrics, publishing or performing rights details, management, booking agent, and attorney information.

Why You Need a Producer

Everyone needs someone they respect and trust as an editor and sounding board. A producer is advantageous as an objective ear and collaborator. It is impossible to listen to multiple mixes and know what sounds right. Besides becoming brain-dead from music played too loud in studio control rooms, often you are simply too close to the project to make good decisions. An impartial producer can help you discern appropriate lengths, styles, and mixes.

Although many artists certainly are capable of producing themselves, I find the best records are collaborations between producer and band. This is because collaboration is not about control. Collaboration is about trust and partnership. You hire a producer to help you record your music in the best possible way—trust them to do so. You hire a producer to showcase your talents in the best possible light—trust them to do so. You hire a producer to make your project as accessible to the listener as possible—trust them to do so.

Your partnership is based on both creative and commercial tenets. It's not enough for you to share similar creative sensibilities if the producer cannot enhance your commercial viability. Most producers record for a specified fee and a small percentage of future album sales. It is in their best interest to present you in the finest manner possible to maximize your potential.

When to Look for a Producer

Consider a producer only after you've made two demos yourself. Studios are seductive with their high-tech bells and whistles. Yet the hushed atmosphere creates an intimidating situation. It's normal to be googly-eyed at first and reticent to ask questions. Instead, spend some time in self-production at an inexpensive studio to understand the recording process. Educate yourself so those machines don't scare you and learn about mic placement, drum baffling, and specialized equipment. It generally takes two trips to a studio to get over the wide-eyed phase and learn how things really function. Give yourself the time to get acclimated and make your mistakes outside the glare of an expensive producer or someone else you want to impress.

If your music is getting a reaction but you constantly hear criticism about the production, get a producer. Can you really be unbiased about your vocals? Or your girlfriend's bass playing? Do you really have the technical skills necessary to record the material optimally? I find the best self-produced records had strong engineers who handled many of the studio details.

Ways to Find a Producer

Look on the back of your favorite CDs to find appropriate producers and engineers. By researching which studios and engineers participated on those records and contacting some of those people, your efforts may be rewarded.

Many great producers began as engineers

*M*any a fine engineer has become a fine producer. **Mike Clink** worked as an engineer with producer Ron Nevison, recording a variety of '80s superstar projects (Heart, Eddie Money, the Outlaws) including three Jefferson Starship records. In the mid-'80s Mike went solo, moved to Los Angeles, took a chance on an unknown band called Guns N' Roses and produced their seminal debut, *Appetite for Destruction*.

I remember Mike not only actually keeping Jefferson Starship's recording schedule on track (at the renown, raucous, and rowdy Record Plant in Sausalito, CA), but also forging a close personal and artistic relationship with the band members. I often thought several band members were more comfortable discussing their music with Mike as their creative collaborator than with Ron, their producer.

Karl Derfler was the engineering partner behind famed producer Jerry Harrison. Karl worked with a host of bands including Stroke 9, Live, and the Dave Matthews Band before he got the nod to produce Smash Mouth and Big Head Todd and the Monsters solely on his own merits. Karl had recorded innumerable unknown bands along the way, perfecting his studio chops and collaborating talents. He remains a truly savvy studio virtuoso.

While you may think it unrealistic to expect that a multimillion-selling producer would be interested in recording an unknown band, everyone is looking for *the next big thing*. Producers often use the large fees paid them to record superstar acts to underwrite their personal projects. If you share the same musical sensibilities, they may like working with you, provided you have the talent, a plan, and can prove you are serious about your career. (Use your gig schedule, Web site, and the corroborated response to your music to validate your seriousness and help establish your worth.)

Consider bypassing expensive producers and talking with engineers instead. Engineers are the most highly underrated sources of production talent. Engineers generally do the majority of work on records, but get secondary credit. Engineers and second engineers are always looking for projects to elevate them to "producer" status. It's well worth your time to research and contact them.

Make sure you choose projects that are slightly above the level at which you are currently working. Working with people who record just a bit better, write a bit better, or perform a bit better generally helps you rise to the occasion of becoming "better."

Rule of thumb: If you contact 15–20 producer/engineers, you will most likely hear back from three to five who will at least discuss the project. Then, possibly one to three will be interested in actually working on a recording project with you.

Fact and Fiction about Radio Airplay

Once you have your songs recorded it's important to get them heard! Radio airplay is the generally prescribed means used to reach the widest audience possible. However, radio airplay is primarily limited to commercial records released by major labels with considerable marketing budgets and staffs. Here is a brief synopsis of getting radio airplay today.

In music business vernacular, the term "promotion" refers *only to radio airplay*. It bears no correlation to promoting a show or an event. Neither does it refer to any aspects of publicity or marketing. It is used strictly as it relates to radio and getting songs played on the radio. A record label promotion rep or independent promotion company services new releases to radio stations for airplay consideration. The promo rep or company follows up with the stations' personnel (program director, music director, or the radio group's regional program or music director) to get the record added to the play list and then moved up in number of plays each week. The more the song is played, the more opportunity for people to hear it, buy it, and go see the band play it live in concert.

Commercial Radio in the Twenty-First Century

Major labels and independent promotion companies handle *all* successful promotion today. If you want your song played on a commercial radio station, you must use one of these two avenues. Since major labels promote just their own releases, the only other alternative is independent promotion companies.

While it is true that most independent promotion companies do have established business relationships with certain stations in certain formats, most commercial radio stations simply will not accept songs for serious airplay consideration unless accompanied by a well-financed, long-term marketing plan. So while you may be able to hire an independent promotion company to present your record to a prescribed list of stations and do the follow-up, you should be aware of how slim your chances of success truly are—despite these companies' claims to the contrary.

The formats of commercial radio most available to independent rock-oriented releases are Triple A (Adult Album Alternative) stations. However, even in these circumstances, be realistic about what success they can actually garner for your project. Just getting added to a play list in light rotation may not be substantial enough airplay to sell the number of records necessary to get the attention of a major label. Getting played a few times a week may not be enough return on your investment to warrant the money you are spending.

Remember, the reason you want radio airplay is to show definitively that your music gets a reaction. Establishing record sales from radio airplay is the most obvious way of showing your music gets a reaction. If you can't actually track sales off your airplay, then trying to get airplay is an ineffective use of your marketing budget.

Radio stations rarely play self-released independent records sent to them. Program directors and music directors are precluded from talking with a self-promoting artist for these reasons:

The sheer number of releases being considered makes it impossible to service everyone. With over 25,000 records released in a year, radio still has only so many slots for music. With the finite time limitations of 24 hours a day and seven days a week, most stations only "add" two to five new records a week, factoring in the other "currents and recurrents" that are being played. This is why independent promotion companies originally became so popular, serving as a filtration process and helping radio focus on more bankable songs.

The commercial relationship a station builds with the label and artist for a cycle of singles is responsible for both that station's popularity and bottom line. If an artist makes a record with three potential singles, this could easily translate to two years of advertising buys from the label plus extensive promotional efforts from the artist (like performing at station holiday shows and summer fests). An artist with a stand-alone single generally does not win the same long-term respect from stations as the labels or artists who can deliver a continual supply of hit music.

Outside programming of playlists by a higher-up group program director is the norm for many stations. If there are several stations in the market owned by the same corporate entity, music is often divvied up among the stations according to narrow format and marketing guidelines. They choose artists who fit the stations' demographic profiles. So no matter how friendly you are with that ostensible PD, he could be precluded from playing your record.

Many bands obtain lists from industry source books and send records out to station program or music directors. This is a total waste of time and money. Save it, and research an alternative route to commercial radio. The acknowledged resources for independent releases consist of college radio, regional public radio, local music shows, and specialty shows.

College Radio

Although college radio is now a format heavily marketed by major labels, its playlists and personnel are open to independent product.

Since most college stations don't have advertising, they are not locked into the cycle of hit song/ad buy/promotional favor that defines the commercial stations. College radio can embrace the more alternative and noncommercial side of music without bottom line worries, while its youthful audience enables more alternative and experimental music to be played.

However, because of the number of CDs being made today, college radio is not a field for the casual independent release, either. Just as in commercial radio, college stations are inundated with product from major labels and independent promotion companies. Additionally, the program directors and music directors are usually full-time students who have even less time to listen to new records. That is why many college stations leave the majority of playlist decisions up to the on-air personnel, after establishing a weekly skeletal list. It's smart to research the specific shows on college radio and service the hosts of shows that are appropriate to your music. Include these hosts in your follow-up calls and promotional efforts.

While it's not mandatory, you can retain a professional who specializes in college radio. This will greatly increase the odds of someone actually listening to your music. There are independent promotion companies that work college radio much like those that work commercial stations, but they are less expensive and specialize in this more fluid market. Review your campaign with them realistically. In college radio, the music industry is impressed only by airplay on stations that are tracked by the legitimate trade magazines. Use your resources most wisely and target college stations that "report" to a trade.

Whether working alone or with a professional, plan out the type of college stations you are going to service and how to do the follow-up to track the airplay accurately. Target a *specific* region so you can do ancillary promotional activities. Limit it to 35 to 50 radio stations, since that's a quantity you can call and follow up on yourself. When you get airplay on any one of those stations, use it to build a small marketing campaign and regional tour developed from that information.

Sending out CDs to 300 college stations around the country is a waste of time if you are not able to follow up productively with cross marketing (such as on air-appearances, in-store retail tie-ins, or live performance promotion). Remember, you want a cohesive strategy where every positive action leads to another positive action, demonstrating that your music gets a reaction.

One misconception about college airplay is that the quantity of stations counts. Maybe it counts if the quantity is in the *hundreds,* but 50 college stations in the middle of nowhere playing your CD in light rotation is meaningless if you can't prove you're selling records or tickets because people in Bismarck, ND, are hearing your music on college radio. If you don't have national distribution and a coast-to-coast tour, your money is better spent on a focused regional campaign designed to achieve specific results.

In realistic terms, college stations are much more valuable for building a fan base, providing an anchor for promotional events, and creating regional buzz. Never underestimate the power of college radio, college crowds, and college towns to create and maintain your band's buzz.

Public Radio, Local Music Shows, Specialty Shows, and Options

Like college radio, public radio is not bound to the same strictures as commercial radio and is fast-becoming another good alternative for independent artists. However, because of the older demographic of most public radio listeners, these stations strongly embrace singer-songwriters or those artists who fall into the Triple A category of literate, thoughtful, skillfully executed music. Certain radio personalities, syndicated programs, and linked public events may lend themselves to your type of music.

In addition to servicing individual program directors, make direct contact with the producers of the various public radio programs. Most shows on national public radio are independently produced efforts whose talent and music decisions lay with the producers and hosts. Since many of these programs are syndicated nationally, try building promotional activities in several of the markets that broadcast the show.

Local music shows on commercial stations are a great way to get DJ quotes for your album, publicize your release, or promote a gig. Note that these shows are not considered real radio airplay and can't be bandied about as such, but they can help you get someone's attention, such as a producer, reviewer, or booker. Local music shows also add to your overall "story" (especially if you get good listener feedback and call-ins) and give you another media angle to work.

Specialty shows exist on commercial radio to air unusual, intriguing, original releases that don't fit anywhere else in the radio genre game. Occasionally a song will test with enough audience response to move over onto the regular playlist. Not only is this rare, it's even rarer for self-released product to even get on these shows. But specialty shows do remain a strong and viable vehicle for the small indie label (i.e., not your own label). And once again, they add fodder to your story and offer an opportunity to create either controversy or conversation about your music.

Options for getting airplay include cable TV music channels, satellite radio, Internet radio stations, and video games. Each of these mediums is looking for fresh content without the traditional limitations. Film and TV placements through music supervisors are also viable outlets for unsigned bands.

Trade Magazines

Trade magazines not only provide comprehensive music stats, they help you understand radio airplay and album sales—the basic principles of the music business—and how they work.

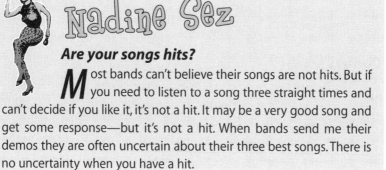

Are your songs hits?

*M*ost bands can't believe their songs are not hits. But if you need to listen to a song three straight times and can't decide if you like it, it's not a hit. It may be a very good song and get some response—but it's not a hit. When bands send me their demos they are often uncertain about their three best songs. There is no uncertainty when you have a hit.

The trades track radio airplay and sales in every conceivable genre. It's important to do your homework and read the trades to understand the ebb and flow of the charts. The most widely read trade magazines are *Billboard* (this Grandaddy of them all has the most meaningful charts because they combine radio airplay and album sales); *Radio and Records* (the gospel for every radio format, this has the truest airplay stats and most information); *CMJ* (if you are working in college radio, it is *essential* to chart on *CMJ*'s reporting stations); and *HITS* magazine (this official industry insider mag is a must for current gossip and politics).

Whether your music is formatted toward commercial or college radio, it's very important to focus your efforts on *reporting* stations. It really doesn't matter where you are getting played unless it's a station that reports to one of the trade magazines. The industry uses these radio reports to scout out new buzz bands, hype product, and sell more records.

Read the trades to find out who is playing like-minded music and which stations might offer a sympathetic ear to your record on their local or specialty shows. Then offer those stations a format-specific song and be prepared with a strong rationale for why they should play it.

The trades are the music industry's "bibles." Read 'em and weep, but read them you must if you are serious about the business. The industry rule of thumb is that you must be in heavy rotation over a period of time to make a dent in the industry's consciousness. The number of song spins equating the number of records sold varies considerably from format to format, hit to hit, artist to artist, and year to year. But the trades help put it all in perspective for you (and for your prospective major label).

Chapter 6 Keywords

1. A **hit song** is any song that gets an **immediate positive reaction**.
2. Spend your demo money showcasing **your songs**—not the CD's production.
3. Find a producer who works as a **collaborator**.
4. **Research** your radio options carefully.
5. Don't **waste your money** on unrealistic independent promotion.

REAL-WORLD SUCCESS STORY:

Counting Crows Demos

Counting Crows are the epitome of a band who recorded their first demos cheaply and prolifically. The result of those efforts—their unique music—ultimately helped instigate a new radio genre.

Early in my preparations for producing a BMI showcase slated for February 1992, an office mate passed me a demo of Counting Crows. The tracks were "roughs" of works in progress from this newly formed band. Lead singer Adam Duritz, guitar player Dave Bryson, drummer Steve Bowman, bassist Matt Malley, and keyboardist Charlie Gillingham had teamed up after stints in other local bands. Adam and Dave were prolific songwriters who wrote fast and furiously. At the time, they co-owned a small recording studio in Emeryville, CA (across the bay from San Francisco), and recorded their new material constantly (with their friend Damian Rasmussen as engineer).

For the first six months it seems they never gave out the same demos twice. Once I asked Dave about "the second song" on the tape I'd just received. He couldn't remember what he had sent me, since they just kept recording fresh songs, rearranging material, and developing their music all the time.

The songs were captivating. They were recorded simply enough to let Adam's delivery and style stand out, yet they were also recorded fully enough to showcase the potential of each song. There was something very, very special about Adam's voice and those song arrangements. The band was as cohesive a unit of players as I had ever heard, and they had forged a distinctive sound.

Rick Riccobono and Julie Gordon, both at BMI at that time, deserve a lot of credit for helping set the stage for this band's signing frenzy. Counting Crows already had a strong management team and favorable legal representation in place and were ready for business. Rick and Julie blazed the potential of this band to all of the Los Angeles industry, touting the uniqueness of the songwriting and Adam's emotional, edgy delivery. The evening of the BMI showcase at the I-Beam in San Francisco, I had a preshow cocktail party packed with industry heavyweights. Even I was impressed to see head of VH-1 John Sykes and friends. The band delivered a set rough in execution but brimming with passion, Adam's confident originality, and Dave's strong vision. The day after my BMI showcase, Counting Crows received serious offers from more than seven major labels and inquiries from another five outfits.

Even more amazing, their characteristic sound helped start a completely new classification of radio station called Adult

A rare shot of Counting Crows performing at my 1992 BMI showcase; the next day the band received multiple record-label offers. The Crows' demos of their unique singer/songwriter-rock sound caught everyone's attention and helped define a new radio format, Adult Album Alternative (Triple A).

Album Alternative, now commonly known as Triple A radio. This new station format embraced the emerging trend of rock bands (formerly played on album-rock radio) who wrote powerful songs (formerly played on alternative radio) with literate, thoughtful lyrics and melody (formerly played on adult-contemporary radio). Counting Crows' songs helped set the musical parameters for this new radio genre. Not many bands can point to spawning a new radio format! What a testament to this band and the power of their original talent.

REAL-WORLD SUCCESS STORY:

Starship—Three No. 1 Songs

Evolving over the years from Jefferson Airplane to Jefferson Starship to Starship, this band demonstrated how to make radio hits over the course of three decades. While I was director of promotion and publicity for Jefferson Starship and then Starship in the 1980s, the latter incarnation of the band had an unprecedented three consecutive No. 1 radio hits. In a significant break from the past, these songs were written by different *outside* songwriters, recorded with different producers, released on two different albums, and ultimately marketed to different radio genres.

The biggest of the three hits was indisputably "We Built This City" (1985), which played on album rock radio and Top 40 or contemporary hit radio (CHR). The original demo for the song sounded nothing like the finished Starship version. The song was written by Bernie Taupin, produced by Peter Wolf (not the Wolf of J. Geils fame), and released on *Knee Deep in the Hoopla*. It also hit No. 1 worldwide.

As soon as the band had recorded the song, it was clear that "We Built This City" would be a smash hit. People deep inside the industry started calling me—*months* before the album was even close to being released—providing the first indication of the popularity to come. And during the life of that song, for more than one year, the constant attention never stopped. Although I never thought it was Starship's best song, it obviously struck a chord across America, in all formats and for all ages.

"Sara" (1986) was a beautiful ballad that showcased Mickey Thomas's great voice and began the band's cross over from legendary rockers to contemporary hit-makers. The song was written by Peter Wolf and Ina Wolf, talented Austrian musicians, who changed the song character's original name to Sara for Mickey's then wife, Sara Kendrick. Peter also produced the song, and it too hit No. 1 in America.

"Nothing's Going to Stop Us Now" (1987) was an excellent duet for Mickey and Grace Slick, and it became a CHR staple. It was written by (now superstar, then struggling) writer Diane Warren and Albert Hammond, produced by the phenomenal Narada Michael Walden, appeared on the soundtrack for the movie *Mannequin,* and received an Academy Award nomination for Best Song. It hit No. 1 all around the world and was the second best-selling single in Europe in 1987. The song also appeared on Starship's album *No Protection.*

I'm most proud of these three consecutive No. 1 hits because I played a pivotal role in orchestrating their radio success and obtaining top chart status.

I was fortunate to work with a gifted RCA staff in what amounted to a three-year team effort. We toured Japan, went to Europe twice, and crisscrossed America playing "sheds," the new outdoor venues that were springing up. We appeared on countless MTV specials (including a live New Year's Eve concert where Ping-Pong balls were dropped from the ceiling into the audience, who picked them up and pelted the band and each other), spring breaks, awards shows, and contest promotions, including one where we rented a boat and rocked out on the San Francisco Bay. Limos, money, and traditional rock 'n' roll fun was abundant.

But in crossing over from legendary rockers to contemporary hit-makers, Starship traded their core rock audience for the more fickle CHR audience. Since the nature of hit radio is song driven instead of band driven, many listeners ultimately quit supporting the band—they were no longer fashionable or recording the songs the fans wanted to hear.

Many harsh critics blamed the demise of this once legendary rock band on the recording of these three hit songs (again, penned by outside writers) and on the demands of the more erratic contemporary hit radio audience. But I know from the inside that Jefferson Starship/Starship had been in an untenable stasis of declining commercial viability and *had* to change with the times. I give longtime manager Bill Thompson huge credit for getting three decades of radio hits and touring opportunities out of this incredibly fractious band(s).

I've always thought the career collapse that came eventually was merely inevitable. The band had—after three decades of worldwide mythical status—simply run their course.

7

Solicit a Manager, a Lawyer, and an Agent

Introduction: The Rules of Attraction

The music industry is a relationship-based business. No artist can do it without the support of a team of music industry professionals such as managers, lawyers, or booking agents. The partnerships you make with these professionals have a direct bearing on your career.

Musicians often make the mistake of thinking these music industry professionals fall in love with their music. But in reality, most of these professionals fall in love with the band's business potential. Of course they need to like your music, but that's taken for granted, just like your talent is taken for granted. Do you have an attractive enough story that will persuade them to invest their time and expertise toward the success of your project?

Everyone forgets that music professionals are simply salesmen or saleswomen who sell your vision to the rest of the world. Are you giving them something they can sell successfully? Are you unique? Are your songs drop-dead memorable? Do you have a stage presence out the yin-yang? Are you selling over 50 records a show, consistently? Does your music get a reaction?

Believing you have written a hit song is good, but proving you have written a hit song that elicits a concrete response is what attracts music industry professionals. Believing you have a dynamic presence is good, but showing the effectiveness of your dynamic presence with consistently sold-out shows is what attracts music industry professionals.

To get the attention of music professionals you must be able to show that your music propels an audience to *take action*. Upon listening to your music, a fan should walk into a record store and buy your record, or call up a radio station and request your song, or buy a ticket to see your live performance, or go to your Web site for more information. When you can show a music industry professional that your music compels people to react in one of these ways, with sustained interest, they will probably become more interested in you.

This chapter will help you understand the different roles each music industry professional can play in your career and which services you really need. You'll also realize that your future manager could be right in your own backyard, and you'll learn some management do's and don'ts. The real world success story will focus on some old school and new school managers I've worked with along the way, who all started as friends and fans of their respective bands.

Understand the Professional Distinctions

Managers, lawyers, and booking agents all play very different roles within the industry. Many musicians have expectations that are not appropriate for the particular professional they hire.

Managers are responsible for overseeing every aspect of your career. They interact with every department of the record label including sales, promotion, distribution, publicity, product management, and A&R. They pursue publishing opportunities for your music. They speak to radio stations; work with independent promotion companies; hire publicists, agents, and attorneys; retain office personnel; oversee tour staffing; and strategize merchandise marketing. They are responsible for the creative, commercial, and fiscal health of your band.

Managers employ road managers, stage managers, and business managers to handle other facets of the band's business. **Road managers** advance the touring schedule; deal with agents, concert promoters, and building managers; confirm travel arrangements and transportation needs; and hire the sound and lighting companies. **Stage managers** supervise day-of-show interaction with the concert venue including all union activities, and serve as the foremen for the lighting company's road crew, the sound company's road crew, and your band's onstage and offstage traveling personnel. **Business**

Nadine Sez

Management time line snapshot

*I*n general, years one to five of the time line consist of bands forming, bands breaking up, new bands forming, making demos, more demos, adding new band members, writing songs, and gigging. In years four through six, things start to gel. You make breakthroughs in the songwriting, the lineup stabilizes, you find the right people, and you begin to know how to record correctly. That is generally about the time you find a manager who begins to recognize your potential, who starts to believe in you and falls in love with your music. After that, it usually takes a few more years to refine the music, make the right demo, find the right showcase, and develop the right relationships to get you to a major label. Upon signing, it usually takes two more years to release a record nationally.

managers oversee the payment of taxes, salaries, and professional dues; handle all insurance needs; establish lines of personal credit; negotiate mortgages; and advise on investments.

It's helpful to consider your manager an extension of your band, since they are *your voice* on every level—from publicists to booking agents, crew, producers, record stores, and the label. A manager is helpful in providing the more detached overview you need to formulate a successful strategy and approach. A manager is also helpful for ferreting out the inside scoop from the label and other industry professionals on what the marketplace is looking for and how to give it to them without losing the band's personality in the marketing process.

A manager is available 24 hours a day, seven days a week, and 365 days a year as a business mentor, therapist, mediator, hand-holder, confidant, confessor, and Dad (Mom). It's rare that a manager is unreachable. This type of accessibility, commitment, and sheer time spent together (rehearsals, gigs, studio, tours, meetings) rivals time spent together in most marriages. My rule of thumb says you "marry" a manager and "hire" a lawyer.

Managers can contact labels and negotiate terms, but they cannot draft a legal agreement or book a gig. Most managers collect 15–20 percent of your gross revenues and recoup their office, entertainment, and travel expenses. Sometimes young bands will pay young managers a monthly flat fee ($500–$1,000) until more traditional revenue streams are established. Occasionally managers will take a higher percentage (most notably Colonel Tom Parker, who took 50 percent of Elvis Presley's earnings). Some managers' fees are written into the band contract as a full member of the band (like Bill Thompson with Jefferson Airplane, Jefferson Starship, and Starship) to ensure greater management incentive and more equitable pay.

Lawyers negotiate deals with labels, draft agreements, and decipher contracts. Their job is to wrangle the best contractual opportunities for you. Lawyers generally don't involve themselves with the artistry of your show, the longevity of your career, or your creative life. They don't help you with set lists, song structures, stage presence, or publicity opportunities. They are only concerned about the number of potential hits you have, because that influences their bargaining position.

A lawyer's most valuable asset is time. You will be billed in increments of 15 minutes, with hourly fees that can escalate into the hundreds of dollars. You do not call your lawyer when your van breaks down outside of Las Vegas and you can't make it to the show. You can pay lawyers by the hour, a percent of your contract, or a prearranged flat fee for services rendered. Expenses are generally limited to office expenditures. Lawyers can call a label to shop a band, but they cannot manage a band or book a gig.

Booking agents are responsible for procuring professional talent for paid appearances. Their only job is to secure paying gigs for your live music act. If you get paid, they get paid. Booking agents are concerned only with the number of people that will come see you play live or watch you on cable TV's Pay-Per-View. They are not concerned with record sales or radio airplay, except for how it relates to your live attendance draw. Booking agents secure contracts for your performances and collect the advance monetary deposits, ensuring your appearance at the venue (as a conflict of interest, managers are forbidden by law in many states to book bands). A booking agent has little monetary interaction with record labels and works almost exclusively with band management.

Define Your Professional Needs Accurately

Initially a manager is necessary only when you have so much business activity going on that you can no longer keep track of your day-to-day responsibilities. This doesn't mean you're just tired of calling the same unavailable club bookers or press reviewers every week. A manager is not the magic balm or elixir for your career. Many bands look for managers too early because they are weary and frustrated. Management is time-consuming work with little hope of any swift, tangible reward or immediate monetary recoupment.

Being self-managed for as long as possible not only helps you appreciate a manager when one commits to your project, but also forces you to learn the business side of music. This is a valuable education for making smart, knowledgeable decisions down the line. No matter what your status, you always want to stay abreast of decisions being made on your behalf. Remember, no one will ever be as responsible to your success as you.

A lawyer, on the other hand, is first necessary when you want band, production, or management contracts drawn up or reviewed for favorable terms. You are ready for a booking agent when you have consistent attendance in a certain genre of performance venues (generally nightclubs or colleges) and wish to expand your geographic base of performing.

When Should You Look for a Manager?

When you have something to sell. Assess realistically what you have to offer a manager that would entice him or her to take you on as a client. Assemble the facts that prove your music gets an enthusiastic reaction. Sell a manager on your possibilities by displaying your past efforts. A manager's love of music is great, but it does not cover his or her basic necessities: office expenses, food, rent, and the kids' college educations. Until you can offer a manager appreciable examples of revenue potential, it will be hard to get current professional managers to be interested in you.

When you can pay. You are ready for a manager when you are willing to make compensation for his or her work. It's worth your while to pay for commitment, professionalism, and dedication. If you are resentful over what you are paying your manager, maybe it is not time to enter into a management agreement. Many bands worry needlessly about the money that might come to them, and then negotiate cheaply with their managers. Twenty percent of nothing is still nothing. Don't nickel and dime your manager—that will take away his or her incentive to succeed on your behalf.

When you are ready to listen. You are ready for a manager when you are willing and able to listen to him or her. Can you listen to your manager and uphold your end of the partnership by providing good songs, good fans, or a good stage show? Can you listen to your manager and make the appropriate creative changes?

A manager tells you the truth about your songs, recording quality, pacing, and arrangement of shows so you maintain a quality product and a competitive edge. If the pacing of the set is poor or the act's just not working, your manager owes it to you to tell you so, even if you disagree about that 20-minute guitar solo or the band personnel. If you are shopping a demo and your songs aren't strong enough, you need to be told. If the sequencing needs to be different or your show needs improvement before you're ready to showcase, you need to be told.

A manager is often the *only* person who *will* tell a band the truth, because everyone else in contact with the band wants to be liked by them (label, fans, crew, agent, attorney). If the manager can't tell the truth, the band may as well quit the biz because *no one else will* tell them the truth. A manager who is unwilling or unable to give a

Nadine Sez

Signing too early can deter a manager

*B*ands often make decisions that unintentionally preclude getting a manager until further down the line. For example, making a deal with an indie label will deter many managers. If a manager likes a band and their songs, he or she will want to take them in and develop them to specific industry contacts. Already having an indie deal will preclude this, because the band's batch of songs is already under contract and will require the manager to pay out or buy out.

Many indie label deals do not require a manager—the money involved is much, much smaller and generally not large enough to share. However, you can use your record sales on an indie label to attract a manager after the fact, because then it will give that manager something significant to tell to his or her contacts.

Even obtaining a major label record deal is a deterrent to a manager, unless you've held some money back to pay him or her. If not, the label deal is done and the money dispersed among the band members and lawyer. Unless you are willing to let a manager shop a publishing deal for you, there will be no money forthcoming to management until after record sales and touring grosses. But due to accounting standards and start-up costs, those sales and grosses are two years down the line from an album's release. It's these bottom line realities that make it so hard to find management.

band a true critical assessment does a tremendous disservice to his or her clients.

When major labels are calling. A manager (or lawyer) is a valuable asset when the major record labels come calling. For the most part, labels dislike talking business with artists directly because it's too time-consuming to track down all the band personnel every time decisions need to be made. They prefer to deal with one person, a manager or lawyer, and let that person get the consensus opinion on business matters.

Also, major labels eventually have to negotiate business terms, but they do not want to offend the artist. The prevailing opinion favors talking music business in an impersonal manner with band representatives who can systematically wrangle for their clients with less emotion.

When your record is coming out. A manager is *absolutely necessary* before the release of a major label record. Your CD will not be the only CD released that year by that label. Signing with a label is no guarantee that they will devote anything beyond the minimum effort to sell your record. No matter how large or multinational, a label's resources are limited in comparison to the number of records that are released. Realistically speaking, a label can promote only so many records effectively.

Before your record is released to the general public, you are battling for your label's time, attention, and money. You want your release to receive the benefits of their promotional and publicity efforts, garner valuable distribution space in record stores, and receive advertising dollars. Record labels spend their resources on records they think will offer a good financial return. It is up to your manager to make sure your band is as attractive as possible to the label to ensure you receive the best promotional efforts.

Before release, a manager must make sure the record has the prerequisite number of singles necessary to excite the label. He or she must make sure the band has a street credibility, generates an industry buzz, and appeals to the significant tastemakers and power suits of the label. A manager cannot let a record come out in the midst of an executive shake-up, company sale, or firing of the label executive who championed the band.

How to Find a Manager

Everyone wishes managers were in the phone book so you could just go to the Yellow Pages and call one. But most of the time the best managers are right under your nose.

One of the biggest myths is that you *must* find a big-name manager to be successful. The reality is that big-name managers are busy with their big-time clients and you will get the crumbs of their time and attention. Most big-name managers simply cannot afford to pay attention to you until you make something happen on your own. Then, they might be able to parlay your efforts into something more substantial.

Consider looking for a manager in your backyard. Look around in your collection of fans and crew. See if anyone has any inclination to take on the job. A dedicated fan who actually understands

A manager should interact with every department of your record label. When I managed Ryan Downe, Rocket Records founder Elton John was very supportive, introducing Ryan to the New York press corps at a fabulous Elton-style party in 1996.

the band, believes in the band, and is committed to the band's music can take you much further than a preoccupied manager who is waiting to see if you make something happen for yourself to warrant their time and attention.

This is not rocket science. Anyone can learn management. There are plenty of advisors and books out there for neophytes. Basically a manager is anyone you trust who doesn't lie, steal, or cheat. A manager should be enthusiastic, willing to learn, and able to devote the time necessary to helping you attain your common dream.

Bad Managers

Bad managers *don't tell their clients the truth* about the reality of the business. A manager who insists on stroking your ego in hopes of keeping you "up" is actually keeping you "down." Oftentimes major label business strategies are out of your control. You should be made aware of the tenuous nature of these business realities in advance. If a label is not going to work your record (possibly because they have too many releases coming out), you need to formulate a different strategy (like holding the record back). Being kept unaware of the accurate situation will impede you from devising a plan that addresses the situation realistically. Knowing the truth will prevent you from making costly and frustrating mistakes.

Bad managers are *reactive, not proactive.* Just like every band must figure out how to get out of the "band ghetto," managers must figure out how to be noticed and effective. A manager should be as creative as the band, thinking outside the box and taking charge of the band's career in creative fashion. A manager who sits back and waits for the band to deliver hit songs, or waits for the label to make decisions, or waits for the booking agent to come up with shows, will probably be waiting for a long time.

Bad managers *don't make their clients work the nonmusic side* of the music business. One of the most important companion aspects of promoting a record is called "meet and greet." Arranged by the label for before or after show gatherings, these opportunities allow the artist to meet and greet the local press, radio, record store employees, and behind-the-scenes movers and shakers. Everyone wants to feel like they are part of a new discovery. As a breaking band, it's your responsibility to reach out to the folks who are actually doing the job of selling, playing, and promoting your records. They are your most valuable allies.

A good management office remembers who you are meeting and why. They often keep notes on pertinent facts to help the artist per-

Nadine Sez

Managers who can't tell the truth

I've always had a hard time telling a band the truth after I get close to them, which makes me a poor manager. There is a very famous singer-songwriter who won multiple Grammys a few years back. I had known about him for years, as he was bubbling under. He won those Grammys after ten years of hard work, finally releasing his third record with strong radio singles. After extensive touring following his post-Grammy success, he went back into the studio to cut his follow-up fourth record.

High on his recent success, he made a record that was intensely indulgent and personal—indecipherable to all but his most hardcore fans. It was completely unfathomable to radio programmers, who refused to play it. He went from having a multiplatinum, Grammy-winning third record to a wreck of a fourth release that bombed in the marketplace, selling fewer than 50,000 copies. This record was trashed mercilessly. Out of frustration over these dismal record sales, he fired his manager, who had masterminded his entire career to date. The manager was an extremely well-liked woman in the business. Her rueful comment after she got fired was, "I should have told him the truth about the record. I should have never let him release that album."

The manager always gets the blame when things don't go right with an artist's career. It's too bad more artists don't accept their own responsibility. If a label is lukewarm about your songs, force yourself to return to the studio and keep writing until one grabs their attention. It *is* a manager's responsibility to help provide you with the tools, inspiration, and assistance you need to produce your best work, but it's *your* responsibility to do that work.

sonalize the meet-and-greet conversations. If a press reviewer loved your lyrics in song three, you can make it a point to mention that. If a radio station added your single two weeks before the official add date, you can be sure to thank them. If a record store created a special in-store promotion around your concert, you can congratulate them on a good job. A smart artist also takes notes for the future, because these press, radio, and retail personnel will continue from job to job in the industry. Starting a relationship with them early in your career can only help you down the line.

Bad managers are *fiscally irresponsible* and do not institute good accounting measures and business management principles. Never trust a manager who says he or she is taking care of everything and not to worry about the money. You should get an accounting of your financial situation every quarter (or six months, at the least), including monies in, monies out, and your tax status (are you paying your quarterlies?).

Today's business managers handle the finances, investments, and taxes for a band. Get in the habit now of budgeting, allocating, and paying taxes. Later, when you do get that $500,000 deal, you won't go crazy and burn through your newfound cash. It's the structure of responsible bookkeeping that is important, not the dollar amounts.

If anyone is ever vague about where the money from your shows is going, or can't explain your T-shirt sales, you should question their abilities. A manager has to know what is going on because he or she is constantly making decisions affecting your money, whether actually touching that money or not.

Professional Checklist

No manager is immune from making the mistake of wanting the artist to feel great. Success doesn't mean one is insulated from these temptations. The pressures of maintaining an artist's ego and keeping the label happy conspire to sabotage management situations over and over again.

A very strong element of faith exists between artists and their music industry professionals. Agreements with them are basically partnerships of trust. Managers, lawyers, and agents trust you to write, record, and perform good songs. You should trust them to take care of your business. If you keep arguing with them, maybe you're not ready for their services or they are just the wrong people for you. This is a team effort and they should be looking out for your best interests.

Ask yourself the following questions before committing to working with music industry professionals, whether managers, lawyers, or booking agents:

1. Are you comfortable talking with them or do they intimidate you?
2. Have you checked out their background to make sure they are appropriate to your music genre?
3. Are they professionally licensed and members of appropriate professional organizations?
4. Have you talked to their prior and present clients?
5. Have you discussed your dreams, goals, and strategies to date?
6. Do you feel they are responsive to your desires or are they dictating their notion of success for you?
7. Does your instinct tell you they are trustworthy and committed?
8. Do they really seem to love the music and know it like fans?
9. Have you asked them what they expect from you and in what time frame?
10. Have you asked them what they can do for you and in what time frame?
11. Have you discussed their fees and payment options, other compensation alternatives, and the criterion for expenses?

Even if you cannot afford a lawyer to draft the contract with your new, inexperienced manager, or to formalize the band's agreement on songwriting credit, *write down all your agreements* on a piece of paper and date it, sign it, copy it for each person, and file the original. It will serve as your legal road map down the line, reminding everyone of agreements made outside the blinding glare of industry interest, in the calm light of a normal rehearsal day.

Lastly, consider working with people who have enthusiasm for your project. If they are capable and can grow into the professional role, don't be seduced by a bigger name. You can always hire business expertise, but you can't buy genuine enthusiasm and belief. Often after signing a band the record label will insist they drop their current manager and get an "approved" manager, much to the band's detriment. I have *never* seen a band fire the manager who got them the deal and then have further success with the label-approved new management team.

Chapter 7 Keywords

1. Work with your **friends**.
2. Hire the **right people** for the **right job**.
3. Make a **commitment** to your **partnerships**.
4. Remember that success is a **team** effort.

REAL-WORLD SUCCESS STORY:

Old School/New School Managers—
Bill Thompson, David Lefkowitz, Eric Godtland,
Tim O'Brien, Robert Hayes

These five managers cover four decades of music business and a diverse roster of bands. But the one thing they have in common is that they all started as fans of the music. In two cases, the bands tried "big-name" managers only to find the outcome disappointing. Each band then looked in their immediate circles of friends, fans, and fellow music lovers for management. Each of these managers may have started in entirely different career fields but were drawn inexorably to the music and the personalities involved. All five of them directed their bands to eventual platinum success.

Bill Thompson, longtime manager of Jefferson Airplane, Jefferson Starship, and Starship, was the roommate of Airplane singer Marty Balin in the early days of Haight-Ashbury. Working as a copyboy at the *San Francisco*

Chronicle by day, he hung out in the city's burgeoning rock scene by night. It was only after Bill cajoled nationally respected *Chronicle* music critic Ralph J. Gleason to come down to the Matrix nightclub on Fillmore Street to watch the then-unknown Jefferson Airplane, that the band's fortunes began to rise. Gleason's prominent review was the break the band needed and it propelled them into local prominence, starting a chain reaction of increasingly higher levels of success.

Before long, Bill had ditched his day job to work as the Airplane's road manager. Marty and Airplane bassist Jack Casady had asked him to talk to the "straight" people. He often found himself making high-level business decisions for the band when their "official" managers (Matthew Katz, Bill Graham) were not available. This included buying singer Grace Slick's contract from Howard Wolf, the manager of her first band, the Great Society. In early 1968, Bill took over the full-time management responsibilities for Jefferson Airplane.

Under his management, various incarnations of the band recorded social anthems, love songs, and chart hits, toured for over 20 years, and sold millions of records. Bill negotiated the industry's *very first* boutique label within a modern record company (Grunt Records/RCA), bought a mansion on the edge of Haight-Ashbury for office and rehearsal space, and finally saw Jefferson Airplane inducted into the Rock and Roll Hall of Fame in 1996. Bill continues to administer the Jefferson Airplane, Jefferson Starship, and Starship catalog of songs.

David Lefkowitz graduated from Duke University with a degree in psychology and thought he might go on to medical school. Instead he moved to San Francisco and started a local booking agency. His roster consisted of his own management acts, a few of record producer David Rubinson's acts, and an assortment of other hot, unsigned bands. David's roster started a scene called "funk thrash" and threw monthly festivals in an Oakland club. When they started selling out these shows (1,200 capacity), David added merchandising items (T-shirts and cassettes) to the program.

In 1989 one of David's clients, Primus leader and bass player Les Claypool, borrowed $3,000 from his father to press 1,000 copies of a live album. Primus started selling the album on consignment locally and David sent 200 copies to college radio stations, charting in the Top 100 of *CMJ*. The band played at the *CMJ* convention and toured the country. They got better distribution and sold 5,000 more copies. Soon they signed a one-album deal with Caroline Records (a very hot indie label at the time, recording such groups as Smashing Pumpkins, White Zombie, and Hole) and sold 50,000 copies nationally while touring with acts like Jane's Addiction and Living Colour. Caroline Records did a lot at college radio, taking the band to the Top 15. Needless to say, the major labels got interested and Interscope signed the band. Primus went on to sell millions of records and became a mainstay of alternative tours like Lollapalooza and Warp.

Initially David and Les did not know each other very well. But after working together for a few years, they became good friends. They are now partners in their own independent label, Prawn Song. After Primus went on hiatus in the late '90s, David continued with Les's solo career (actually introducing him to a host of creative new projects) while running a full-roster management company and label.

Eric Godtland met Stephan Jenkins of Third Eye Bind through some girls they both dated. At the time, both were interested in film, as Eric was writing a screenplay and Stephan was attending film school. Eric was also spinning records as a club DJ. When Stephan saw Eric's record collection, he mentioned he was a singer-songwriter-musician. Eric listened to Stephan's music and was amazed at his talent. They decided the quickest route to success would be to make Stephan a music star first, then go into film. As Eric says now, "What I thought would take six months took six years."

With Eric serving as his unofficial advisor, Stephan got a song on the music compilation CD of the red hot TV show *Beverly Hills 90210*. Stephan parlayed this initial success into a management contract with a very prestigious Los Angeles management firm that had a large roster of best-selling, cutting edge artists. Stephan was confident this would propel his career forward. In reality, the managers were busy with their more popular artists. They did not have much time to devote to a scrambling, unsigned artist with a minor hit song on a TV show. Dissatisfied with their disregard, Stephan left their roster.

After a bit of time went by, Eric realized that he was already serving as the de facto manager of Third Eye Blind. While Eric had no prior entertainment management experience, he was perceptive and bright. It didn't hurt that he had an MBA from Stanford University. He also had about $65,000 of credit card debt invested in the demo project, as the band's angel investor. So Eric took over the formal reins and they created a dynamite partnership that is thriving today. I've always been impressed by the respect Eric and Stephan have for each other. They have deliberately tried to anticipate every possibility of success and failure within their business plans. By dreaming in the largest but specific ways, they have challenged themselves to reach higher production levels and avoided the pitfalls that sabotage many working relationships. Besides the multiplatinum successes of Third Eye Blind, they run a successful business of band management, studio activities, and merchandising projects.

Tim O'Brien had no prior management experience prior to taking on Stroke 9. As a student at the prestigious University of California at Berkeley, he saw one of the band's shows and went up and introduced himself. After graduating with a degree in business, he joined Bill Graham Presents, the famous concert production company. Although he wasn't working in the management division, he watched, listened, and learned outside the limelight (and pressure) of that division.

Tim made valuable contacts at Bill Graham Presents while shepherding Stroke 9 along the artist development path, and was smart enough to be patient. Biding his time, he waited until the band had all of their ducks in a row before he made the big run. Stroke 9 had one solid single and two more potential hit singles, certifiable independent CD sales, a creative and entertaining press history, touring experience, and a reliable, enthusiastic fan base that bought their records and concert tickets.

When Stroke 9 was ready for a major attorney and a major label deal, there was no doubt in my mind that Tim was ready to be their big league manager. He had grown exponentially with the band and was ready for the responsibilities at hand. Through Tim's astute guidance, the band parlayed one single, "Little Black Backpack," into a radio monster, ensuring two years of steady record sales and worldwide touring opportunities.

Tim is now concentrating on his newest rock talent, Michael Lee and the Rising (on Maverick Records), while expanding T.O. Management. I won't be surprised to see him as a label president someday...he definitely has all the right stuff.

Robert Hayes was a guitar player for a rock band in San Jose, CA, before morphing into a manager. After years of playing in clubs, he realized he was on a dead-end path as a rock star. He searched for another way to stay in the music business. His savvy business experience and his empathy for striving musicians provided him a perfect entree into the world of music management.

Sensible and down to earth, with good business acumen, Robert bridged the seemingly disparate worlds of rehearsal halls and record labels with ease. He was also smart enough to establish a working relationship with well-respected Los Angeles lawyer Kim Guggenheim. Although Robert did not know the musicians who would eventually become Smash Mouth, they had heard of him through other bands he was managing. One day, singer Steve Harwell showed up on Robert's doorstep, looking for management. At that time, Steve had a hip-hop project, FOS. Robert was able to get Steve a solo deal with a minor label, Scotti Brothers. But before the record could be released, Snoop Dog came out with his hip-hop record and changed the style of the genre forever. Steve's record was never released.

Meanwhile, guitarist Greg Camp and bassist Paul DeLisle were playing in a rap-rock group called Lackadaddy. Steve asked Robert to introduce him to Greg, saying he wanted to start an alternative rock group with him.

Robert made the introductions and the musicians began writing and playing together. Steve's vocal personality was the perfect vehicle for Greg's strong songwriting. As different as all the band members' personalities are, it was instant karma, as they say, and the rest is a history of classic hits, national success, and constant exposure. One of the first songs they wrote was their breakthrough "Walkin' on the Sun," which appeared on their debut album, *Fush Yu Mang*. Their second CD, *Astro Lounge,* contains their biggest hit so far, "All Star," which, to this day, has no burn factor. The brand-new (as of this writing) album, *Get the Picture?,* sounds to my ears like it will continue Smash Mouth's string of radio hits and fan favorites.

With Robert as manager, Robert and Steve are now partners in Spun Out Records. Robert has also shown special astuteness in licensing Smash Mouth songs to advertisers and garnering placement on choice soundtracks (*Shrek*). He never misses a cross marketing opportunity, using as many different media outlets (retail and fast food tie-ins) as he can to promote the band and keep them in the public eye. Smart, smart, smart. He also runs a management company with a variety of acts, including the Fighting Jacks, Drist, and Watashi Wa.

Criteria for Record Labels, Publishing Companies, and Performing Rights Societies

Introduction: Assessing the Current Label Situation

I've watched the music industry survive several doomsday scenarios over the past 20-plus years. Instead of making me blasé or jaded, this witnessing makes me excited. One of the most attractive qualities of the industry is its chameleonlike ability to change, evolve, and adapt to current demands and trends. Because it is a business model whose bottom line depends on shifting audience moods, the music industry is in perpetual mutation. This nonstasis is exactly what ensures opportunity and possibility for anyone who is willing to take a risk, whether that risk is selling records or making records.

I've lived through folk music, blue-eyed soul, Motown, Chicago blues, acid rock, British rock, hippie rock, '70s rock, disco, new wave, punk, '80s rock, grunge, Triple A, metal, urban, rap, new age, and electronica. Industry crazes come and go, predicated by album sales. The prevailing flavor of the day can demand prerequisites today that may be passé tomorrow. The industry machine moves very slowly, usually several years behind the street trends that drive it. This is all the more reason for you to have established a distinctive personal style of creativity that can serve as the bedrock of your career.

If your music gets any kind of reaction at all, there will always be someone out there willing to try to sell it for you. The criteria for *who* may get signed *when* may change, but *someone* will always be willing to gamble on the potential reward of having hit records.

There is much debate regarding the disparate benefits of DIY (Do It Yourself) projects, indie labels, and major labels. As a major label collaborator, I believe in the business of selling and promoting records on a grand scale to a large national and international audience. Regardless of which aesthetic appeals to you, meeting the criteria for major labels will maximize your options for having a career within parameters you have defined personally.

This chapter will give you specific guidelines for speaking with major record labels and courting their interest. Today's competitive and crowded marketplace dictates a very high standard of creative and commercial savvy rendered in a strictly proscribed manner. That's why indie labels or DIY projects remain options, either as stepping-stones to larger success or permanent homes for more personally manageable success.

Submission Guidelines for Major Labels

The importance of iPods and other Internet-driven listening devices is steadily increasing, which is why you want your best material on your Web site, or teaser snippets. Most reps still want a disc to play in their car while commuting or for their DiscMan or iPod while jogging. While they could burn a CD off the net, I

Nadine Sez

Signing without management

If you don't have a manager when you sign a deal, be sure to reserve some of your advance as an inducement for the manager of your dreams. Although they may not have *secured* the deal, you will be asking them to *work* the deal, and they must be compensated accordingly to have enough incentive to do a good job.

Labels want to perpetuate the myth that they respect artists, so they are openly hesitant to talk about marketing dilemmas, song selections, and creative issues with artists directly. They prefer to deal only with lawyers and managers on a band's business issues so they can speak frankly and directly. Indie labels, on the other hand, look to develop relationships with artists directly and sometimes actively discourage bands from management. Either way, a manager is a convenient buffer for creative or financial hassles.

Major labels have a multitude of releases vying to be "worked" by the label. To be "worked" means the labels put their full energy (i.e. staff and money) into getting radio airplay, getting the record into stores, marketing, and publicizing the product. Because of staffing issues, availability of retail space, airplay feasibility, marketing dollars, budgets, and personnel, a label is only working about five records at a time (out of many releases.) The rest of the releases are basically thrown against a wall to see if anything sticks. Your manager must go to the label and fight for your record to be worked! Your manager must beg, plead, threaten, and cajole to make sure you receive those precious marketing and promotion dollars. This is definitely a situation where the squeaky wheel gets the grease (providing the band has created a record that is workable, containing hit singles and selling potential—not some lame product that they insist on releasing because of their egos).

advocate sending reps your own manufactured CDs, complete with your artwork, to help them get a well-rounded view of your creativity. You can also easily combine your songs, a press kit, and even a video on the disc. This ensures that reps have all your valuable information on hand for reference.

However, *never send unsolicited material* to a major record label. Most do not accept it, and your lovingly created CD will be treated like trash! One standard justification for not accepting material blindly is the fear of liability in a plagiarism lawsuit. The more honest reason is that the numbers of music demos submitted is truly daunting. However, labels do want your music and use only a modicum of screening to sift through submissions. If you can get someone vaguely professional to recommend your music, they might listen.

The key is to get introduced to someone in the A&R department. It won't do you any good to become best friends with someone in the business affairs office, a product manager, or the local promotional rep because they rarely have any input on A&R activities.

Introductions can come in many different ways. Label A&R reps take pride in having their ears to the ground with voluminous street connections. Label reps talk to local writers, recording studios, record producers, engineers, record store managers, attorneys, club bookers, booking agents, managers, friends, and other bands about *who* is doing *what*.

An artist can use one of these avenues to get a referral name at a label. Call the recommended contact and state how you got his or her name and number. Tell the contact a bit about why your music would be of interest and ask if you can send your demo. Only *after* obtaining the okay, do you send it. Remember to indicate your three best songs if you are sending a full-length disc.

You can cold-call an A&R department and talk to an intern, receptionist, or scout when you have something significant going on with your career. This is a good way to start a dialogue with the A&R department. Phoning regularly with career information will go a long way toward establishing your commitment. E-mail updates and newsletters are important, but I prefer the additional rapport a phone conversation provides.

A manager can call labels and introduce him or herself without needing referrals, but introductions are always preferable. The best calls are made by referencing a mutual associate and offering solid facts about the band's recent successes to hook the A&R staff into listening to the music. However, simply establishing a connection with a label rep can begin a valuable exchange of information, critique, and advice that will help a manager continue to develop an artist's talent while initiating industry relationships.

Lawyers can call labels, "shop" your music, and negotiate your record deal as an alternative to a manager. At different times in industry history, attorneys have facilitated at least 50 percent of band signings, though the trend seems to be swinging back toward managers. As mentioned before, lawyers are not hand-holders like managers. Attorneys will make a deal and walk away.

Look at the backs of CDs to see who is representing whom. If your music is up to par, these attorneys may want to represent you—they *are* in the business of making deals, after all. It's very hard to cold-call lawyers due to their time constraints, but most will take your call if referred from another client, manager, band, agent, or producer.

Six Criteria for Major Labels

No one gets signed after one enthusiastic phone call or e-mail missive, or after a demo is received and listened to in the A&R office. Too often bands expect an immediate response to the music they send to a label. It takes label reps some time to get through a stack of requested submissions and complete daily professional obligations. Give them one to two weeks before you follow up with a call or e-mail.

If a label rep likes your music, then a *lengthy* process ensues, beginning with an assessment of your complete music output and potential. Then your commitment, stability, personality, and track record of activities to date are assessed. The rep will research your Web site, live performances, and album sales. He or she will speak at length to your manager, attorney, and possibly your support staff, and will research your regional contacts and local connections. Ultimately the rep will consider whether you'd be a good creative fit for the label without overloading the roster in one particular genre.

Lastly, the label rep appraises whether you'd be a good investment for the company. Each of these valuations is used to convince the core label executives or executive committee of your benefit to the label.

There are six benchmarks used to help evaluate your potential to a label. Generally you need *two or more* of these to be considered seriously.

1. **Fantastic songs** (three potential radio singles)

Good songs are simply not enough in the current major label marketplace. You need *great* songs and preferably three songs perceived to be potential, radio-ready hit singles. The reasons are numerous, but here are two that I mentioned earlier in Chapter 6.

First, it costs major labels a minimum of $500,000 to promote a record's first single (add in the album costs and ancillary costs, and you are over $1 million to break a band). Having invested that much money, the label is hoping for a *second* single to push album sales over $1 million so *they* can start making some money. Your manager is desperately hoping for a *third* single so *the band* can start making some money (earnings up to that point may be applied to the label's recoupable costs of making, promoting, and selling the record, which are deducted by the label from the record sales—before the artist gets paid).

Secondly, radio professionals are looking to build relationships with artists who they can help become stars. If they help make them stars, then they can ask the artists to play their station's Christmas, anniversary, and charity shows. They can do this with artists who give them a series of singles, which also ensures a series of ad revenue from the major labels. It's symbiotic, but the bottom line is reality. Radio pros will generally not waste their valuable time and short play list availability on one-hit acts.

With the tremendous losses in recent years due to money spent on making and releasing records, labels are now rethinking their commercial strategies. I predict a rise in small personality-driven labels that are fiscally conservative yet creatively liberal, hearkening back to the days of Island and Chrysalis. This, however, will not negate the necessity of radio-driven success. Radio continues to become an indispensable tool for niche marketing.

2. Manager or attorney

You *must* have a manager or attorney to negotiate the deal. Either one works, but it's very, very rare for a band to get a major label deal themselves, since labels want a management system in place to get the necessary jobs done. Most labels will not talk actual business with artists directly. When artists do secure contracts for themselves, the label immediately asks them to find a manager to coordinate the myriad aspects involved in making, releasing, and selling a record on a national scale.

As discussed in Chapter 7, having a manager is absolutely necessary before your record is released on a major label to ensure it gets the proper marketing attention and promotion respect.

3. Compelling live show

Do not confuse a *compelling* live show with a *polished* live show. A compelling live show insists that the audience members put their drinks down, stop hitting on those babes, and pay attention to the show, the band, and the lead singer. Experienced professionals know live shows can be polished through professional direction and incessant touring experience, but the one thing you can't teach, buy, or sell is charisma and the ability to "own the room." Star presence is palatable, even in its roughest forms.

4. Solid local following

If you are as great as you say, then where are your fans? Bands must have some sort of fan base, generally drawing over 300 (at least) to impress anyone in the business. Major labels are looking at you as an investment. They are looking for proof that you can sell through a live performance. A local or regional draw tells the industry that you have enough presence, songs, and vibe to get people to respond to you by coming to the shows. This proves you are marketable. It gives the label the footing for a breakout marketing campaign.

5. Certifiable Internet presence

Start tracking users' hits to your Web site so you can present real numbers showing the effectiveness of your music campaign. Be prepared to give out commercial Web sites' sales figures. Be ready to show your value on the sites that rate and test records. If you're not on the Internet today, you will be at a distinct disadvantage with a major label.

6. Certifiable independent sales

If you can sell records, you don't need a live show, press kit, or any other ancillary prop to get ahead in the business. The key is certifiable sales. Many bands proclaim to sell "a lot, man," but how many is "a lot"? Fifty; 200; 500; 1,500; 15,000? The manner in which you sell is not as important as the total sales numbers, so you can sell through multiple outlets like record stores, the Internet, and at your live shows.

If you say you sold 1,000 records, you must authenticate it. Today, bands can sell 1,000–3,000 records as a matter of course. Five thousand in sales is attractive and will get a music professional's interest. But the watermark is really "10,000-plus CDs sold." If you can say and prove you've sold 10,000 CDs legitimately, a major label will be seriously interested in you. It means you already have a certifiable fan base for launching a national campaign.

The industry employs a commercial tally system called Soundscan as their standard of tracking record sales. Soundscan can track any bar coded CD for a fee, regardless of source (major label, indie, or DIY). They also can track the CDs you sell at shows, which is a service worth paying for if you are selling enough CDs to warrant the cost and can meet their criteria. Using the established but varied commercial selling Internet sites (Amazon.com, CDBaby, CDNow, Acteva, Paypal) is also advisable because they track your sales transactions automatically.

If you develop just one of these criteria, you will find more options available to you. It's so costly today to promote bands that everyone is looking to minimize the risk—even indie labels and DIY projects.

Options to Major Labels

An independent label (indie) is just one option to a major label. Indies come in all shapes and sizes and can offer a less stressful, more personalized fit for wider creative palettes. Indie labels range from established genre leaders to garage operations. Financial support, promotional and marketing support, and distribution capabilities vary from indie to indie.

Independent labels also have closer, more casual relationships with their artists and are generally more approachable. Bands are encouraged to call and develop relationships with label personnel. The criteria for indie labels are as mandated as that of major labels, but use a different priority system based on similar musical tastes or kindred lifestyles. Because there is less monetary investment, the stakes are not as high and often the reward is more immediately tangible. Independent labels that cater to a specific audience can be successful, money-making operations with proportionally higher payoffs to the artist than a major label.

Conversely, the staffs and resources are smaller, so more of the work is dependent on the effort you are willing to make on your own behalf. As an indie artist, you are competing with better-funded, better-staffed companies for the same newspaper review space, the same record store bins, the same radio time, the same Internet audience, and the same live fan base.

DIY (Do It Yourself) projects are another alternative to a major label. Rising in popularity, these are CDs released by the artists themselves, or tours promoted by the artists themselves. The artist is responsible for recording, manufacturing, artwork, distribution, sales, promotion, publicity, and marketing costs in their entirety. The return is immediate. Middlemen are kept to a minimum or eliminated. You have total control in defining the scope and possibilities of the project. By nature, DIY projects have smaller prerequisites for success. If you manufacture 1,000 CDs and sell those, you've sold out! If you sell 1,000 tickets, you've sold out! There is no obligation to succeed on someone else terms.

The disadvantages with DIY are that you are competing not only with major label resources but also with indie label credibility for that same newspaper review space, same record store bins, same radio time, same Internet audience, and same live fan base. However, certain niche genres of music makers, like touring jam bands, alternative college bands, punk bands, explicitly gay or lesbian groups, and electronica/dance acts, are busting the business open with their "take charge" business attitudes. Unwilling to give their business away to major labels, they are creating innovative Web sites that foster online communities of fan(atics), provide instant chat opportunities and insider band information, sell tickets, sell merchandise, and offer immediate concert downloads. Without big mark ups and huge promotional costs, these bands are finding they can service their fans respectfully *and* make a good living by touring six months out of the year. Bands like String Cheese Incident, STS9, Ani DiFranco, and Big Head Todd and the Monsters come to mind as good examples of DIY.

DIY is also an excellent way to get started, to learn the business from the ground up and get your feet wet in the actual *business* of the music business. It's valuable for helping you discern your personal, evolving definition of career success. Then, when you have established yourself enough to have major labels become interested in you, your business model will be so well formed that you can negotiate with a businessperson's mind instead of an artist's mind.

The Publishing Alternative

Publishing companies can be terrific alternatives to approaching major labels. They are an underused resource in the music industry today. More concerned with artist development, a publishing company will spend time and resources helping a potentially valuable songwriter develop. If you have good songwriting chops, they are an extremely viable entrée into the music business and can help support you through your development.

Publishing companies are in the business of songs. They buy the rights to songs or portions of the rights to songs written by songwriters. They then sell those songs to other artists for recording purposes, commercial use in film, TV, or advertising, and other mercantile avenues. As the songwriter, your songs are the actual currency of a publishing company. This is a tremendously powerful position from which to negotiate.

Once you get over your fear of losing ownership of your published songs (an urban myth), an extremely collaborative creative and commercial relationship can be established. In today's sophisticated business world and all the avenues for self-education, there is little to fear of someone stealing your publishing like the horror stories of the 1940s, '50s, and '60s. Publishing companies are also more flexible in offering an array of different business arrangements, from single-song deals to multiple-year deals. Standardized contracts can be tailored to fit your situation more easily at a publishing company than at a record label.

A good partnership with a solid publishing company can provide not only tremendous assistance with a recording career (the publisher can help you get a record contract after establishing your songwriting credibility), but also enormous cash value because of the film, TV, and song-pitching resources. Depending on the strength of your material, the company will take your songs to film and TV music supervisors, album producers, and A&R reps, when appropriate.

When you get frustrated with responses from record labels, consider a publishing company as an alternative. They don't care about your local following, your stage show, how your demo is produced, or whether you have a marketing strategy or plan. They only care if you have good songs. Melissa Etheridge, Stephan Jenkins, and Teitur are just a few of the artists who obtained publishing contracts before major label record contracts.

Contact a publishing company in the same manner you contact a label. Research them to find out which companies represent which songwriters. Find referrals through other musicians, lawyers, managers, producers, studios, and songwriters. Call before you send any material.

Differentiating among the Performing Rights Societies

BMI, ASCAP, and SESAC are the performing rights societies. These companies license the *right* to use their vast repertoire of songs in all public circumstances. Radio stations, TV shows, film companies, Internet sites, concert halls, bars, restaurants, jukebox retail stores, elevators, and phone services all pay established fees for the right to use your songs as entertainment or background music. The performing rights societies negotiate your compensation, collect the levy, and disburse the money among their members. Each society uses a complex system to track your song usage, ensuring equitable payouts. Although each society employs different accounting programs, there are enough industry checks and balances to make their respective song disbursements quite similar in size and scope.

BMI and ASCAP both operate as nonprofit companies. Outside of their minimal operating expenses and small general reserves, all of the money collected is dispersed to the songwriters and publishers in their repertoires. SESAC is a "for profit" society that is privately held and has the smallest roster of songwriters. All three societies deal exclusively with songwriters and publishers.

You do not need to sign with a performing rights society until your music will be played in a commercial medium, such as on radio, TV, a film soundtrack, or a jukebox. Most self-released DIY records do not warrant signing with a performing rights society. Major and indie label releases do warrant it.

Benefits of the Performing Rights Societies

The societies can be good sources of information regarding licensing and royalties. Their Web site content and magazines can help you understand the maze of industry paperwork. They support an array of conferences, conventions, and educational seminars designed to assist the aspiring songwriter. They sponsor songwriting competitions, new music showcases, songwriter nights, and compilation CDs that can help give you visibility and start a buzz. The writer-publisher reps can help you with referrals to publishers, labels, managers, and attorneys if your material warrants it.

The BMI showcases I produced in the 1990s under the aegis of Rick Riccobono served as launching pads for many a future artist. Bands like the Beauty Stab (who went on to become the Dandy Warhols), Candlebox, Counting Crows, Third Eye Blind, Train, and Stroke 9 all went on to major label success. Showcased acts like the Sextants, Sister Double Happiness, Inspector Luv and the Ride Me Babies, Seven Day Diary, Psychefunkapus, Paul Durham, and Cola all got signed to major labels only to get dropped from the label's roster when they failed to sell enough of their debut records.

Think of performing rights societies as the best of both worlds. They are collection agencies with an artistic purpose. They are actually protecting your artistic rights by collecting your money. They are also in the forefront of copyright defense, royalty protection, and Internet collection.

Advantages of Music Associations

Music associations like the National Association of Recording Arts and Sciences (NARAS, the Grammy Awards organization), National Association of Songwriters (NAS), and regional and local songwriting

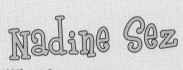

Why I favor BMI

*F*ounded in 1940, BMI is an American performing rights society that represents approximately 300,000 songwriters, composers, and music publishers in all genres of music. Through its music performance and reciprocal agreements, it grants businesses and media access to its repertoire of approximately four and a half million musical works from around the world.

I'm proud to have been a longtime consultant to BMI, the world's largest performing rights society. I have only the highest respect for CEO Frances Preston and the staff she has carefully assembled. I can tell you firsthand that the BMI staff is responsive to your needs. Frances has shown incredible strength of purpose in shepherding not only BMI but also the industry through the challenges of recent cutting edge technology. Her remarkable vision has ensured these breakthroughs are used to the benefit of the music industry, artist, and audience.

BMI has always been first at protecting and advocating for musicians. Historically speaking, BMI was created to represent disenfranchised country and African-American musicians. The organization has continued to be on the forefront of every new development and was first in tracking college radio and licensing Internet music. They have instigated protective copyright legislation and stimulated national and international debate on collection and rights issues. Why be second when you can be first! To get more information go to www.BMI.com.

associations are a wonderful support structure for the aspiring artist. They are good for making new contacts and meeting other artists. They help you understand the music business through conferences and seminars. And they are a safe place to explore your calling.

Chapter 8 Keywords

1. Realistically assess whether or not you can **meet the criteria** demanded by major labels.
2. **Consider options**, such as indie labels, DIY projects, or publishing companies.
3. **Use** music associations and source books to your own advantage.
4. Explore the **Further Reading and Index** in the back of this book.

REAL-WORLD SUCCESS STORY:

Stephan Jenkins and Third Eye Blind

Third Eye Blind is a good example of a band that worked for years refining their sounds and experimenting with different personnel until they had the right combination for major label success. The independent route was never an option for lead singer and bandleader Stephan Jenkins. He always wanted—and ultimately achieved—mainstream success.

Stephan has always had a tremendous sense of self-confidence. Among his many talents, I think this is his most attractive trait. I'll never forget when he walked into my office—a total unknown—sat down at my desk, and proceeded to tell me how to run my showcase! I wasn't mad. I was amused at his seriousness. He has never been shy about going after what he wants.

Even in the early stages when his career stalled due to early industry management and band difficulties, he would pick himself up after every setback and reapply himself to his

---

chief objective of getting a major label deal. Self-confidence generally garners a bad name, but I think it's an absolute necessity if you want big time commercial success.

Stephan was able to get a small taste of success when he and a songwriting partner scored a minor hit on the *Beverly Hills 90210* compilation CD. He quickly signed with a big league Los Angeles management firm and proceeded to be ignored. He returned to San Francisco licking his wounds but with a better sense of what was needed to sustain the industry's interest. He capitalized on his nascent five minutes of fame with a publishing deal, which supported him while he wrote songs and played around the Bay Area, testing several variations of band personnel.

When Stephan met bass player Arion Salazar (whose band Fungo Mungo had been signed to Island Records), he knew he had found a musical soulmate. With Eric Godtland already committed to the team, these three created the nucleus of Third Eye Blind. Guitar players and drummers came and went, but when Kevin Cadogan joined on guitar and Brad Hargreaves on drums, the lineup was fairly intact.

Attending the BMI Pop Awards in 1998 with Third Eye Blind manager Eric Godtland, lead singer Stephan Jenkins, and his date, actress Charlize Theron. Before they connected with fame and success, Jenkins and company worked hard to find the right musical combination for 3EB.

It was at this time, in mid-1995, that I asked Third Eye Blind to headline my BMI showcase for a local music conference. They were one of the hottest bands in the city and there was no place for them to go but up. The Paradise Lounge was packed the night of the show, and I had bands performing on three stages (including Cola, who went on to sign with Epic, release a record, and disappear). Although 3EB played a strong closing set to a roaring crowd, nothing of substance materialized immediately for the band from the industry.

Bolstered with confidence but impatient, Eric, Stephan, and the band decided to use Eric's money to make a great demo with a professional engineer, then hire an expensive, powerful attorney to shop the record. The band had rearranged a song that Stephan had written called "Semi-Charmed Life" and with the new arrangement they thought they finally had their "hit" song. Six months and $65,000 later they had a demo engineered by then unknown producer Eric Valentine. After meeting with several firms, they hired an attorney in New York who specialized in new artists and shopping demos.

To help the process along, the band arranged a hometown showcase concert at the Fillmore in San Francisco, with other local faves Stroke 9 and Black Lab (both of whom would go on to garner record deals of their own, on Universal and Geffen respectively). Unfortunately, that night was plagued by technical difficulties and Stephan had the flu. Their drummer quit and the crowd was hostile. It was basically a nightmare show, and yet another big opportunity came and went. Stephan's publishing option expired and was not renewed. Things looked bleak.

Not losing faith, Eric, Stephan, and the lawyer continued to meet with labels. At one meeting, Stephan challenged a label rep to let Third Eye Blind open for Oasis in San Francisco. The rep called his bluff, and 3EB faced a sold-out crowd of rabid Oasis fans a few weeks later. Much to the surprise of everyone except Stephan, the band not only won over the crowd, they were demanded back for a raucous encore. The concert promoter was so impressed he paid them double the agreed-upon amount (this *never* happens).

Third Eye Blind played a showcase in Los Angeles where Sylvia Rhone, the head of Elektra records, happened to be in attendance. Sylvia had heard the demo from the attorney and the songs had stayed with her. The set bowled her over. Over the objections of her A&R staff, she signed the band. Released in spring 1997 and buoyed by the single success of "Semi-Charmed Life," their first album sold over three million copies in little more than a year! When this book went to press, 3EB had just released their third record, *Out of the Vein,* and had plans to tour extensively through the remainder or 2003.

REAL-WORLD SUCCESS STORY:

Meet A&R pros Rose Noone and James Dowdall

A&R is really a team effort based on guts and instinct. Two A&R pros who have always followed their instincts are Rose Noone (senior vice president at Epic) and husband James Dowdall (senior vice president at Warner Bros.).

When I first met Rose and James in the early '90s, they were driving around the US in a van looking for bands for Chris Blackwell's Island Records. James, an Irishman, had moved to London in the mid-'80s and went to work for Stiff Records before moving on to Island Records. He made a name for himself by licensing the unknown band Nine Inch Nails before they hit it big. Rose had worked in New York City booking a small club before moving to London and falling into a video/marketing job at Island Records. After she and James hooked up, they became a working team, with James scouting the acts and Rose filming them.

In the early '90s, Chris Blackwell sent them to America with the vague, open-ended directive to wander around looking for and filming bands. Starting out from New York City, their first stop was Columbus, OH. In quick order they had gone from Columbus to Cleveland, Cincinnati, and Louisville, before setting out for Denver. Before they got far, though, they heard about a buzz band in Dallas called Tripping Daisy, so they rerouted themselves to Texas. Upon arrival they immediately went and saw the band play to 1,000 crazed fans in a Dallas nightclub, complete with lines out the door and raves from record store and radio personnel. Rose and James fell in love with Tripping Daisy. They called Chris Blackwell the next day to tell him they had found him a band. They had been in America five days.

That auspicious start landed Tripping Daisy for Island Records (Island's release sold an incredible 10,000 records a week with absolutely no MTV airplay—unheard of at that time) and set the tone for James's and Rose's fortuitous career based on instinct, guts, and a commitment to hard work. Other notables they have signed together are Tracy Bonham (James offered her a deal the first night!) and Macy Gray (they agreed to move to Los Angeles for the duration of her recording process…eight months later they were just getting to the mixing stage!).

James left Epic in 2000 and went to work for Warner Bros., where he found an unknown San Jose, CA band called Trapt, whose debut has already gone gold (over 500,000 copies) and is still rising. Rose remained with Epic. Besides signing the hot new act Howie Day, she continues to work with Macy Gray while overseeing other projects on the roster like Fiona Apple and Tori Amos.

Both Rose and James agree that the scouting process starts with the songs, and then they look for uniqueness in an act. As James once told me, "The first thing that grabs my attention on the radio is the vocal…music is a very nonintellectual art form…you have to really feel it…."

9

Practical Advice to Go

Introduction: Nadine's Wild Wisdom

No one gets it right the first time out of the box. Musicians start as fans and acolytes. Label executives start as interns and assistants. Managers, lawyers, and agents start as concertgoers and record buyers.

In the course of a career there will be moments of great joy and happiness. You will feel a sense of deep accomplishment and satisfaction in the efforts you've made. You may even make some money. You will also experience depression and lethargy when things seem to be moving too slowly or not at all. At times, you may feel betrayed by your friends, the audience, business reps, or artistic muse.

The more versed you are in your rhythms of making a living creatively, the more open you will become to the process. Soon your desire to create and your actual manifestation of that desire will be just a normal part of your life.

If you are called to express yourself musically, or called to work with musicians or the musical rewards of their efforts, the following 12 points of wild wisdom are worth reflection no matter where you are in your career.

1. The No. 1 Problem Is Frustration

The No. 1 problem with music is not the big, bad music business—it's frustration. Frustration causes bands to break up, solo artists to stop performing, singers to stop singing, and songwriters to stop songwriting. If you stop creating, you can't get signed to a label that can help your music reach hundreds, thousands, maybe even millions of people. That's why the entire process is about not getting frustrated and not stopping.

Instead of getting frustrated, empower yourself with information

Nadine Sez

Staying hip—Jason Newsted and Elton John

I love artists who stay creatively active year after year of their lives. Two artists I've been fortunate to interact with, who epitomize staying current, are bass player Jason Newsted, from the bands Metallica and Ozzy Osbourne, and Elton John, the true King of Pop. Both are rock war-horses who have shown us how to be established yet remain contemporary. I think the secret to their continual individual successes is that they constantly reach out to younger players and younger scenes to keep their creative juices flowing.

It's become somewhat of a tradition for Jason Newsted's current musical project to close my four-day music festival, Nadine's Wild Weekend. The first year he did so, he debuted his first project since leaving his longtime band, Metallica. The new project, Echobrain, consisted of Jason and two guys in their mid-twenties, Brian Sagrafena and Dylan Donkin, making fantastic music as a big, swirling power trio. All the Metallica band members and producer Bob Rock came out to see Jason and wish Echobrain well.

The second time Jason closed the Weekend, he played with his totally improvisational punk-metal band, Papa Wheelie, which features that will continue to propel you forward while cutting down on time-wasting, transient activities. It takes patience to hit pay dirt. Be patient. Have heart and stay your course.

Take a stand to be an artist. Something better will happen in your life—I guarantee it—because you will be recognizing different sensibilities, instincts, and ways to communicate, interact, and function.

2. Every Overnight Success Is Years in the Making

There's no such thing as overnight success. It takes years to refine your craft, define your sound, determine your identity, establish a core support system, and lay down the groundwork that will sustain your success. You also will have acquired the skills necessary to cope with success when it comes to you.

Jason on lead vocals and lead guitar. By the time you buy this book, you probably will have seen Jason out on Ozzfest blowing your mind with his savvy bass playing. But it's his open-mindedness to new musical styles and avenues that I respect most about Jason.

I went to several of Elton John's Oscar parties in the '90s as a guest of Rick Riccobono from BMI, and they were a gas (especially the time I kissed Muhammad Ali on the cheek). But I also met with Elton when I managed artist Ryan Downe, who had a contract with the short-lived revival of Elton's Rocket Records in the mid-'90s. Besides working with Ryan creatively during the recording of his project, Elton was also gracious enough to personally introduce him to the New York press and music industry at a special CD release party. Although Ryan's record and Rocket Records failed when they were caught up in boardroom politics, Elton's interest in the current music scene never diminished. I remember Elton telling us that he regularly went out and spent hundreds of dollars on new releases. He loved being up on what was happening and seemed genuinely interested in new music. Even today his outreaches to new acts like Eminem and John Mayer are prime examples of how he remains current, modern, and aware.

Curiosity may be your most powerful ally in your fight against outside forces stultifying your internal creative juices. Learn from the pros and bring your most curious, creative self to every opportunity.

The same is true for not only musicians, but for managers and support personnel. I remember manager Bill Leopold once told me how to transition from part-time music business to full-time music business. He said whether you were an artist or manager, you made the change incrementally. First you spent 90 percent of your time on your day job and 10 percent on music or business. Slowly that percentage would change as you changed the emphasis in your life. Soon you were devoting all your time to your music or business and neglecting your day job. That was the sign you were ready to move into the situation full-time.

Give yourself the gift of time.

3. Believe in Yourself

No matter what you want to do, you can accomplish it. Believe you are possible. Your belief influences how other people view you. Like attracts like. Success builds on success. Confidence feeds on itself.

Backstage at Nadine's Wild Weekend 2001, surrounded by Jason Newsted and Echobrain, his first post-Metallica band in its first appearance. In addition to his bass-playing skill, Jason knows how to keep his career energized by reaching out to new musicians and fresh scenes.

Use realistic criteria for evaluating not only your talent but also how determined you are to attain certain levels of success. It's important to make a decision with the best information possible and then move forward. Don't be paralyzed into inaction. There is no right or sure way. The key is to keep moving forward.

Art is not necessarily defined by commerce. Define your goals on your own terms, even if you can't clearly or tangibly explain them to anyone else. Give yourself the gift of time to allow your thoughts to formulate and expand. Respect your artist muse. Respect yourself.

4. Be Smart and Trust Your Instincts

Pay attention to your gut. Trust your instincts. Follow your intuition. Everyone has that nagging little voice inside that is always trying to get you to listen to it. *Listen!* That little voice inside is *never* wrong.

Follow your intuition and you will never have to second-guess the decisions you make in your life. It's only when you fight your instincts and talk yourself out of doing something that self-doubt comes into play.

When you put off calling a manager, it may be that your inner voice is telling you you're not ready. Possibly you have nothing to offer them, your songs aren't ready, or your live show isn't up to par. It's to your advantage to *not* make that call until you have the information they will want to hear, and your intuition is telling you this. Don't be afraid to circle the block a few times before making the next step.

You're never too old, too big, or too rich to trust your instincts.

5. Quit Sabotaging Yourself

Good plans demand the ability to recognize your creative cycles. Be flexible in taking the time to regain your equilibrium when necessary. Artists are vulnerable to mood swings. One day you feel like a million dollars and the next day you want to crawl into a closet. Listen to your creative cycles and let them dictate your pace.

When fear threatens to overwhelm you, consider lowering your sights. Sometimes we think we are ready for more challenging endeavors when actually we're not. When you have trouble making that phone call or setting up that meeting, it's usually because you're just not ready to proceed in that direction. Refocus on some concrete activity that is successful in a tangible way (booking a good show, finishing and e-mailing your newsletter) until the time comes when making that phone call seems natural.

Dwelling on missteps of the past is a waste of time and energy. Who is to say they were missteps if you learned from the experience? Let it go and keep moving forward. Looking backwards prevents you from seeing all the opportunity in front of you. If you do something silly, stupid, or horrifying, remember we've all been there.

Learn from your experiences. When you've gone through a bad time with a creepy manager who gave you a bad name, use the experience to rewrite your criteria for your next manager. Instead of dwelling on the time the band was late for the gig, create a new schedule that distributes responsibility for setting up the shows equally. Instead of railing about the junkie guitarist who sold your equipment out from under you, reassess your requirements for band members.

6. Say Yes to Opportunity

Focus on your goals, your message, and your sound. Develop a sound that is uniquely you, and describe it accurately and concisely. Present your image sharply and crisply. Think of two sentences to describe your music and a tag line to identify yourself. Write down your goals with time line checks.

With this focused approach, you'll be alert enough to say yes to the opportunity in front of you. After concentrating so completely on long-range goals, sometimes we miss the immediate opportunities. Goals, plans, and success criteria change on a regular basis. We often get offers that we refuse because we are looking beyond them. Bill Leopold tells an insightful story about why Melissa Etheridge signed with Rondor (Almo-Irving) publishing and why she signed with Island Records. "Those were the only two parties interested in us—they were the only ones to offer us a publishing contract and then a record contract."

Commit to working with the people who *are* interested in you now, not the people you think *should be* interested in you. Quit thinking you always know what is right for you or what is the right path to success. Inspiration and success work in mysterious ways. Just say yes!

7. **Be a Professional All the Time**

Maintain a professional attitude at all times. You never know when that club doorman may become a label president. In this age of monthly start-ups, you never know who may be watching and looking for someone just like you.

Treat every show like it's Carnegie Hall. There may be a budding journalist in the crowd who could write up a show review. There may be an engineer looking to move up with a new project. Or there may be a bored manager looking for a new act.

Everyone you meet on the way up, you'll meet on the way down. People who work in the music business have a tendency to stay working in the business. Be careful how you treat people when you're on top. Things always change.

8. **Work with Your Friends**

Put your friends (who show a committed interest) and other like-minded people on your team. It's important to have a good support system that helps you have fun and enjoy your work. If you can't work with the people you like most, work can become draining and demoralizing.

Spend your time developing business relationships with compatible people who encourage and inspire you. Since musicians spend a disproportionate amount of time on their music together, it's important to spend it with people they appreciate and trust. The friends you have now will be the friends you have for a long time.

Contact other artists. Artists like other artists, despite varying success levels. Art and creativity have nothing to do with success. It's the mutuality of ideas and the creative sparking that is so attractive.

Don't hold back because someone is more successful. Stay connected with your fellow artists regardless of stature. It's a myth that superstars work only with other superstars.

9. **Think Outside the Box**

In music, the playing field is wide open. Anything goes and anything is possible. Think outside the box when it comes to promoting yourself and be open to novel, creative ways to get in front of your audience. The bigger you think, the bigger your success can be. Don't let yourself be put off by negativity from other less successful, less goal-driven musicians.

Make your creative muscles work to your advantage in business situations instead of taking the easy way out. If you came up with a terrific bridge, you can come up with a great new location for your shows. If you wrote a haunting melody, you can write an arresting bio of the band. If you attained the exact sound you were looking for in the studio, you can find the right words to explain yourself to a label rep.

10. Take Responsibility for Your Career

Be responsible for your own destiny. Don't wait for it to be handed to you, or you will be waiting a very long time. Be conscious of the decisions you are making and accept responsibility for them, good and bad. There is little that we can control in this world, but you *can* control the decisions *you* make.

Be proud to be an artist. Step into the role wholeheartedly and tell people who you are and what you're doing. How can others find you if they don't know who you are? If you stay grounded with belief in yourself, plus have your time line and strategic plan, all else will fall into place and you will end up exactly where you're supposed to be!

Don't be content to let the vagaries of the business dictate success or failure to you. If you suffer setbacks, work to circumvent them creatively. Don't rely on just one aspect of the business for your peace of mind. I've seen musician after musician get a record deal, only to be devastated when their records neglected to sell and they were dropped from the roster.

Let's face it: There are many, many musicians who have had horrific major label experiences. But if you're talented enough to get signed, then you already have the valuable tools necessary to reformulate a plan. Self-motivation is often the difference between a career and a disaster.

11. Embrace the Process (It's a Passion, Not an Obligation)

Honor your passions. Do what you love and live the happiest life possible. By honoring your passions you have an excellent chance of avoiding regret. It's the process, not the end result, that is called living. Hopefully your music career will be fun, enjoyable, and rewarding for you in many ways impossible to predict.

I see too many people taking this too seriously. This is life, love, fun, and adventure. It's not supposed to be a day job or a corporate job (although it demands as much work!). It's music. Live a little and quit being so serious! Everyone thinks they have to have a hit, sell records, and make money. Well, yes, that would be nice—and this book has offered you guidance on how to do that—but really, isn't having fun and enjoying what you're doing equally important? Isn't giving it your all, knowing you took the challenge, and having no regrets despite the outcomes ultimately what is satisfying?

You can make a great plan and write great songs, and you still may not get recognized. If success is the only thing that is going to make you happy, you may be in the wrong business. We are *all* worth more than the results of our best efforts.

12. **We Are All Collaborators and Colleagues**

All business is about partnerships. Label personnel, managers, and agents are your partners and collaborators in success, not your enemies. If you have that "us against them" mentality, then you've chosen the wrong people, label, band mates, path.

Everything you do is collaboration. When you sit down to write a song on the guitar or the piano, that is collaboration between your muse and the instruments. When you co-write a song with another person, that is songwriting collaboration. When you record in a studio, that is collaboration between you, the recording technology, and the engineer. When you perform live, that is collaboration between you and the audience. When you call a club booker, that is collaboration between your ability to perform well and the booker's ability to provide you the platform to perform.

Never feel you are outside the loop or someone knows more. Someone may be more experienced, but it is still collaboration of information that is shared. We are all collaborators and colleagues in this thing we call the music business. From the muse to the soul, no one does it alone.

Nadine Sez

On the subject of greatness

Many people have asked me what it takes to be great. How can you become the next Miles Davis, Howlin' Wolf, Janis, Jimi, Who, Stones, Beatles, Van Halen, Pearl Jam, Nirvana, Guns N' Roses, Nine Inch Nails, Madonna, Michael Jackson in the '80s, Bruce, Eminem, Elvis (both of them), Beck, or Beastie Boys? Greatness isn't given—it's achieved.

And the truth of the matter is: No one starts off great. How can you? It takes time to figure out who you are and what makes you uniquely you. What feels right for you? What is your message? What is your heart? What is your soul? It's your uniqueness that you package up and sell in the guise of new hit songs or musical styles.

You start by defining attainable goals, like playing a local club on a weeknight. That is an attainable, tangible goal that moves you from A to B and gives you credibility to move on to C. It gives you the chance to write and rehearse songs toward a goal. As simple as it might seem, this must be your main goal at this point in your career.

You just have to keep redefining your goals so you can accomplish one while moving on to the next. Of course all anyone thinks about is the money, fame, fortune, sex, drugs, and rock 'n' roll—but no one is great in the beginning. People can be stupid, silly, awkward, and clueless in the beginning. That's okay. It's necessary.

This is why every overnight success is maybe ten years in the making. It takes that long to refine your craft, define your expression of your craft, and lay down the groundwork that will sustain your success and get you into people's mindsets. The competition to make people aware of you is so fierce that it takes five to seven years to get in front of the industry on the A&R side, and another two to three years to get to the other departments before you even hit the general public.

One reason you budget, record, play, tour, promote, and do it again over and over is to develop a routine that helps you handle it when you *do* get that recording deal. You'll actually know what you're doing and won't be fazed by the expectations of success and the work ahead (man, the brutal part comes *after* you've been signed).

The reason you build your fan base from 50 to 200, from 400 to 650 to 1,000, is so it becomes a natural progression. All of a sudden (where did the time go?) you're playing in front of 10,000 fans just as easily and effortlessly as you played in front of 500. And if that guitar string breaks, you actually know how to handle it, and you know how to handle people coming up to you after a show, and all the rest that success brings.

The only path to greatness is hard work, belief in yourself, honing your talent, and stepping off the cliff in a big leap of faith. Greatness is usually a combination of toughing it out, talent, confidence, and just plain luck. But if you set yourself up and lay the groundwork, at least you'll have a shot.

"Great" people have usually developed and discarded several different personae and projects before they hit on the right combination. That's called artist development. Hit songs aren't written right away— they are written after a ton of "good" but not "great" songs.

If you are an indie band with a 12-month time line working backwards to sell 5,000 CDs and you stick with the plan—remaining focused but flexible to market conditions—then at the end of those 12 months, whether you have sold those 5,000 records or not, *I guarantee* you will have written at least one bona fide hit song, you will have developed a core attitude of "bandness" that is visible and sustaining, and you will have intrigued an entirely new set of people who are ready to take you to the next level.

That's how you get to "greatness."

Good luck, baby dolls!

End Note:

Writing This Book Was Like Making a CD

After working closely with musicians for more than 20 years, I finally got to the other side of the fence where I had to wrestle with the demons of creativity. I wish every music industry professional had to go through the experience of writing a book, recording a CD, performing live, or painting a picture for public viewing. If they did, they would never ask you those irritating questions about your project ever again! I have more respect now than ever before for musicians and fellow creatives.

I found writing this book was *exactly* like making a CD. First, I decided to use my professional experience to create a seminar on the music business for musicians (I took a stand as an artist). I had to write the content (songs) for my presentation (initial live gig). Then I had to work on my delivery and presentation (overly long set list, poor pacing). Once I polished my delivery somewhat, I thought I had enough for a book (CD). I wrote and arranged and rewrote and rearranged the book (rehearsed songs) over a period of two years while maintaining my other business (my day jobs—consulting with bands, Nadine's Wild Weekend music festival, and speaking engagements).

My first outline was seven pages (song fragments). The next was 22 pages (melody snatches), and so forth as I continued to refine and refine again what I was trying to say (demos and more demos). I had four complete rewrites reviewed by a trusted colleague or two (30 songs recorded for a 14-song CD, remixed and re-sequenced four times), trying to find the right tone and information to deliver (is this chapter a hit song?).

My writing started out as a book of bullet points with attitude (three-chord punk-rock) but developed into high-minded concepts saturated with information (big, bombastic rock songs). Once I thought I was finished, I had to sell it (shop a demo). I had to write a publishing proposal that sold the book (one-sheet bio, Web site, and press kit). Once I sold it, I worked with an editor (producer) who helped me realize my content would be better if I rewrote it in a more full, narrative style (melodic pop songs). Finally, a copy editor (engineer) went through the manuscript and helped me make it grammatically correct and polished (sequencing and mastering).

After I finished writing the book, I had to deal with conversations and compromises familiar to anyone who has ever made a record for a label. Discussions ensued about content (songs to leave on or take off the record), book cover (album cover), publication date (promotional strategies), and marketing ideas (how to sell the album). I committed to a series of book signings (in-stores) and other marketing plans (publicity opportunities).

How time-consuming writing this book became! It took much longer than I anticipated (years), as I sandwiched it between other activities. It took all my belief, discipline, commitment, and energy to bring the project to fruition. I got absolutely sick of answering the same inane questions that I myself had posed thoughtlessly to others thousands of times in the past: "What are you working on?" (The book....) "When will the project be finished?" (I don't know....) "How's the book coming along?" (Fine....) Then they would start over in the *same* conversation: "What are you working on?" Chrisajiminy!

I got brain-tired and bone-tired, frustrated with people, stymied by my dryyyyy spells, and cranky with the incessant interruptions of everyday life. But somewhere in the process I learned my own rhythms, I learned to trust those rhythms, and I learned to take pride in small but decisive accomplishments. When it came to finally turning the book in, I became curiously reluctant and wasted months finishing up some piddling changes, unwilling to let it go. That was a new and valuable creative lesson for me.

This has ultimately been the most rewarding experience to come out of my rock 'n' roll life! I wrote every word of this book, and I'm proud. Now that I'm finished, I can't wait to start on my next book.

Further Reading

Backbeat Books offers an array of "How To" books for the aspiring musician. I recommend all of them, especially Moses Avalon's *Confessions of a Record Producer.* You can also read Backbeat's allied Music Player Network magazines (*Guitar Player, Frets, Keyboard, Bass Player, EQ)* for artist interviews, lessons, and gear information. Many musicians also like *Mix* and *Electronic Musician* magazines.

Donald S. Passman's *All You Need to Know About the Music Business* (Simon & Schuster) is the one book to have in your library if you are interested in contracts and terminology. It's written in a text-dense but readable style that explains a variety of contractual situations and other scary music business terms like "points" and "sync rights."

Music trade magazines like *Pollstar, The Network Magazine Group,* and *Billboard* also publish an array of directories listing record labels, managers, lawyers, venues, agents, publishers, and attorneys. Too numerous to list here, you can go to their Web sites to find the specific directory you need. The *Music Business Registry* also has several different directories including one devoted exclusively to A&R personnel for all labels. *The Musician's Atlas* is also a good resource, but remember to do your homework and target appropriate contacts.

Jay Conrad Levinson's *Guerrilla Marketing: Secrets for Making Big Profits from Your Small Business* (Mariner) is an excellent book for alternative marketing ideas and is packed with all kinds of out-of-the-box thinking. Julia Cameron and Mark Bryan's seminal work, *The Artist's Way: A Spiritual Path to Higher Creativity* (J.P. Tarcher), can help you unlock many internal creative keys and find a broad framework for self-expression (it helped me!).

Here are some other resources to help you on your journey to creating, performing, and selling your music.

Writing and Performing

Jeffrey Pepper Rodgers, *The Complete Singer-Songwriter: A Troubadour's Guide to Writing, Performing, Recording & Business,* Backbeat Books.

Rikky Rooksby, *The Songwriting Sourcebook,* Backbeat Books.

David J. Moser, *Music Copyright,* ProMusic Press.

Recording

Jon Chappell, ed., *Digital Home Recording: Tips, Techniques, and Tools for Home Studio Production,* Backbeat Books.

Mitch Gallagher, ed., *Make Music Now: Putting Your Studio Together, Recording Songs, Burning CDs, and Distributing Online,* Backbeat Books.

Ben Milstead, *Home Recording Power!,* Muska and Lipman.

Huw Price, *Recording Guitar and Bass,* Backbeat Books.

Gear

Dan Erlewine, *Guitar Player Repair Guide: How to Set Up, Maintain, and Repair Electrics and Acoustics,* Backbeat Books.

Scott Hunter Stark, *Live Sound Reinforcement: A Comprehensive Guide to P.A. and Music Reinforcement Systems and Technology,* MixBooks.

Business

Jeri Goldstein, *How To Be Your Own Booking Agent and Save Thousands of Dollars,* New Music Times.

Quint Randle and Bill Evans, *Making Money Making Music: The Musician's Guide to Cover Gigs,* Backbeat Books.

David Wimble, *The Indie Bible,* Big Meteor.

Services, Events, and Info

I conduct **personalized, one-hour mentoring sessions** called BANDAid over the phone for all musicians (or their support team) regardless of where they are on their career paths or where they live and play music. The hour is devoted to assessing and developing your career while giving you practical A&R advice. *Call me!* To make an appointment, e-mail me at nadine@nadinecondon.com.

I also conduct **seminars** based on the tenets of this book, *Hot Hits, Cheap Demos,* and the experience of my long career. Go to www.nadinecondon.com for the current seminar schedule and more information.

If you are interested in finding out more about **Nadine's Wild Weekend** four-day music festival for California music, go to www.nadineswildweekend.com.

Photo Credits

Photo by Jay Blakesberg: page 12
Billy Douglas, Pat Johnson Photography: pages 31 & 49
Billy Douglas, BD Photo: pages 54 & 154
© 2002 Kelly Castro: Page 84
Courtesy of Steve Bowman: page 108
Courtesy of Rocket Records: page 121
Courtesy of BMI: page 147

Nadine's Mantra

Be Kind • Tell the Truth • Be Creative • Volunteer Your Time
Don't Be Afraid to Ask for Help • Don't Be Afraid to Give Help
Thank God • Respect Life • Laugh • Think Big • Live Expansively
Be Forgiving • Be Responsible for Yourself • Be Real
Support Community • Have Fun

Please consider donating to your favorite charities.
Mine are Mission Hospice Inc. of San Mateo County,
www.missionhospice.org;
the Michael J. Fox Foundation for Parkinson's Research,
www.michaeljfox.org;
and Ronald McDonald House,
www.rmhc.com.

Acknowledgments

Dedicated with gratitude to Honey and Howard, my two big-headed boys. I couldn't have written this book without them. Honey has always believed in and supported my writing talents.

Many thanks to the following people, especially my editor, Richard Johnston, Amy Miller, Julie Herrod-Lumsden, Kevin Becketti, Nina Lesowitz, Kate Henderson, and everyone associated with Backbeat; Ian Crombie of West Coast Songwriters (formerly NCSA), who first gave me the idea for the book; Mike Molenda at *Guitar Player* magazine for giving me the editorial direction and encouragement I needed; the late Rose Frager for taking me seriously enough to send me her copy of how to write a book proposal; my dearest friend Marsha Armstrong for reading early drafts; Foster Johnson for being my writing ayatollah; Mission Hospice Inc. of San Mateo County, where the idea that I could begin to speak/write about what I know to be true first germinated; and Sean McConnell (for paying me to write—who says rock, roll, and church don't go together?).

Much love to my families, both the Condons—Kathi, Judy, Lana, Rick, and Mikki (my publicist in training), and the Parsons—Jane, Sandy, Lee, Kathy, Jack, Lyn, Susan, and Al; the grands, the great grands, and all the out-laws and exes; those who are gone but not forgotten...my wonderful Mom and Dad, Grandma Mary, my sister Linda, Shep, Denny, John, Uncle Paul, and Aunt Flo; my San Francisco family (Mary, Sam, Marc, John, Bill, Melani, and Ioan); my NWW homies—especially Caroline Rustigian, Jocelyn Kane, Jay Siegan, and all the Dream Teams throughout the years; all the Swanhuysers—Dee, Peter, Hiya, Jesse, Jane Dawson, and Jonathan Hunt; Sammy Jo and Beau; the Kentucky gang at Zeke's and

Kentucky Derby parties (Go Cards! Go Cats!); photographers and friends Billy Douglas and Pat Johnson; Denise Johnson; Linda Siddall; Karlyn Bennehoof; Patricia Castagnola; Arne Frager; Gaynell Rogers and all the Muffs; Priscilla Thorner, Sue Finn; Pinky Gonzales, Helen Volhontseff, and Katrina Markarian; and my community at St. Bart's Catholic Church.

With deep appreciation to all my industry friends and associates over the years including everyone at BMI, especially Barbara Cane, Hanna Bolte, and the L.A. office; Becky and Alibob; Debby Dill; Jon Blaufarb; Rose Noone and James Dowdall; John Coon and Dal Booth; Gary Falcon; Robert Hayes; Tim O'Brien; Eric Godtland and Stephan Jenkins; Rick and Margo Riccobono; my friends at Provident Financial Services and Jason Newsted; Sarah McMullen; Dan Weiner; John and Eva McCrae; Nick Gravenites; Bill Thompson and all my Starship associates, especially Jacky Sarti; Susan M. Duryea; Andy Allen; Bob Catania; Randy Miller; Don Bernstine; Mark Niederhauser; Rick and Mary Ann Koenig Dobbis; Roxy Myzal; Craig Chaquico; Rena Shulsky; Bill Leopold, Mark Graham, Carter and Catherine Castro; Andy Olyphant; old friends Johnny Barbis and the late Dino Barbis; sweetheart and "go to" guy Patrick Jordan; Mark Davis (finding your Raider ring helped me to trust my instincts); Mr. DIY himself, Bruce Haring; Dave Stroud; Raz Kennedy; both Her Majesty the Baby and Ryan Downe (who both made stunning debut records); and Yavette Holts, who never got the credit she so richly deserved for keeping so many local SF bands on the path.

Last but not least, to the thousands of bands I've had the pleasure of seeing, working with, or listening to over the years! Rock on, roll on, and be on. You've got one life. Live it to your highest ability.

To anyone I've forgotten, my apologies and I'll get you in the next book!

About the Author

Twenty-year music business veteran Nadine Condon has been instrumental in the success of some of today's hottest acts, with 14 gold and platinum records from artists like Smash Mouth, Stroke 9, and Melissa Etheridge. Through the '90s she showcased up-and-coming bands like Counting Crows, Third Eye Blind, and Train, and she continues to help artists develop their potential through her signature music festival, Nadine's Wild Weekend, as well as her private mentoring service and seminars. Condon is a resident of San Mateo, California.

Index

ESSENTIAL TOOLS FOR PLAYERS, PERFORMERS AND PRODUCERS

When you're a serious player, performer, or producer, it's your life. And the Music Player Network has a magazine for you.

The Music Player Network creates magazines for nearly every player in the band. And when it comes to recording, the **Music Player Network** is defining the future for home-based music production, professional project, or commercial studio work. Wherever your musical interests lie, **Music Player Network** magazines are the authority, written by editors and writers who are experienced session players, songwriters, performers, teachers, authors, lecturers, recording artists, remixers, sound designers, engineers, and producers.

Check out the **Music Player Network** magazines at www.musicplayer.com. Get the latest product news. Subscribe online. Enter our Giveaways. Be part of our Forums communities. You can even buy the CDs we review at www.musicplayercd.com

Music Player Network
A division of Untited Entertainment Media, Inc.
2800 Campus Drive, San Mateo, CA 94403
Tel. 650-513-4400 Fax 650-513-4642
www.musicplayer.com

CMP
United Business Media

WHEN IT COMES TO MUSIC, WE WROTE THE BOOK.

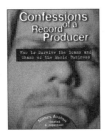

Confessions of a Record Producer
How to Survive the Scams and Shams of the Music Business
By Moses Avalon

If you're a musician, producer, engineer, or any other recording professional, this practical, provocative guide will help you protect your rights and assets. Using real-life examples, this book reveals how producers dip into budgets, artists steal songs, labels skim royalties, and other unfortunate truths—and how you can survive them.
Softcover, 274 pages, ISBN 0-87930-660-2, $19.95

The Complete Singer-Songwriter
A Troubadour's Guide to Writing, Performing, Recording & Business
By Jeffrey Pepper Rodgers

This is the ultimate guide for the modern singer-songwriter, full of real-world advice and encouragement for both aspiring and accomplished troubadours. Interviews with artists such as Joni Mitchell, Ani DiFranco, and Paul Simon offer invaluable insight for the journey from idea to song to stage and studio.
Softcover, 208 pages, ISBN 0-87930-769-2, $17.95

The Songwriting Sourcebook
How to Turn Chords into Great Songs
By Rikky Rooksby

This easy-to-use reference guides novices and experienced tune-smiths alike through the steps needed to put together creative and musically effective chord sequences for any section of a song. A specially recorded CD of full-length instrumental tracks illustrates many of the techniques in the book.
Softcover, 192 pages, ISBN 0-87930-749-8, $22.95

The Gigging Musician
How to Get, Play, and Keep the Gig
By Billy Mitchell

This solution-packed book developed from real-life experiences includes detailed articles on specific problems in gigging, backed by first-hand interviews with musicians, agents, and others who have solved these problems on the road and in the studio. You get practical advice and keen insight on everything from controlling stage fright to controlling finances.
Softcover, 158 pages, ISBN 0-87930-634-3, $14.95

Behind the Glass
Top Record Producers Tell How They Craft the Hits
By Howard Massey

World-class producers share their creative secrets and nuts-and-bolts techniques in this collection of firsthand interviews, offering tips and tricks you can use in the professional or home studio. From creating room treatments to choosing a song's best key, get the inside scoop from the pros behind the glass.
Softcover, 328 pages, ISBN 0-87930-614-9, $24.95

Make Music Now!
Edited by Mitch Gallagher

If you're starting to set up a home studio or making one better, here's all the info and inspiration you need. This is a fun introduction to using computers to make and distribute original music—from the basics of MIDI to choosing and using gear, burning CDs, remixing, marketing your music online, and more.
Softcover, 208 pages, ISBN 0-87930-637-8, $14.95

Backbeat Books

AVAILABLE AT FINE BOOK AND MUSIC STORES EVERYWHERE, OR CONTACT:
6600 Silacci Way • Gilroy, CA 95020 USA • **Phone: Toll Free (866) 222-5232**
Fax: (408) 848-5784 • E-mail: backbeat@rushorder.com
Web: www.backbeatbooks.com